DEVELOPING
AUTHENTIC LEADERS

JENNIFER JENSEN

Tellwell Talent
www.tellwell.ca

ISBN
978-1-77941-545-5 (Hardcover)
978-1-77941-567-7 (Paperback)
978-1-77941-258-4 (eBook)

TABLE OF CONTENTS

Introduction vii

Characteristics of an Authentic Leader 1

1   Leadership 2
2   Authentic Self 5
3   Playing to Your Strengths 8
4   Recognizing Your Weaknesses 11
5   Expectations for Yourself–
    Do They Need to Be Adjusted? 14
6   Life Priorities 17
7   Boundaries 20
8   Stress, Worry, and Control 23
9   Dealing with Hurt 26
10 Passion 29
11 Contentment 31

Leadership Traits to Be Authentic 35

12 Humility 36
13 Integrity 38
14 Vulnerability 41
15 Self-Discipline 44
16 Endurance 46
17 Compassion 49
18 Generosity 51
19 Discernment Mixed with Knowledge 53
20 Consistency 55
21 Reputation, Significance, Legacy, and Talents ... 57
22 Self-Awareness 60
23 Truth-Telling 63

Inspiring Dynamic Teams 67

24 Creating a Positive Environment 68
25 The Value of Knowing Your People 70
26 Motivating People and Team Building 72
27 Building Trust in Your Team 75
28 Building Trust with Your Stakeholders............. 78
29 The Reality of Office Politics.............................. 80

Communication 83

30 Communication 84
31 Nonverbal Communication 87
32 Reading Body Language 89
33 Written Communication 92
34 Active Listening.. 94
35 Dealing with Conflict 96

Influencing the Direction of the Team 99

36 Expectations for Your Team–
    Do They Need to Be Adjusted?...................... 100
37 Be the Calm in the Storm............................... 102
38 Lead by Example 105
39 Be a Follower 107
40 Adaptability..110
41 Decision-Making/Decisiveness........................112
42 Delegating 115
43 Defining Your Success......................................117
44 Ownership and Responsibility 120
45 Dealing with Change 122

Insights That Can Make or Break Leaders........125

46   Being Strategic 126

47   Critical Thinking 129

48   Creative Thinking............................ 132

49   Vision, Mission, and Values 134

50   Meetings.................................... 136

51   Be Organized/Time Management................. 139

52   Negotiations 142

Information Tidbits 145

Tidbits 147

Acknowledgements 155

Notes 157

INTRODUCTION

Inauthentic leaders create a disruptive and negative culture within an organization, as employees lose confidence, trust, respect, and their passion to follow this type of leadership. The organization is typically marked by high turnover and a lack of drive and innovation as well. Organizations want certain types of leaders who follow their ways, which does not necessarily allow for authenticity. Many senior leaders have left organizations, and those left behind often don't have the tools to guide others, especially the new leaders who potentially are missing key components required in leadership.

Did you know …

- Companies tend to focus on maximizing profitability and business tangibles rather than investing in the people and their development. Yet when people are supported and develop their skill sets to achieve their career goals, loyalty, job satisfaction, and self-confidence increase. Turnover is significantly reduced, which is more cost-effective for the organization, as people's passion and drive are realized. It costs more to replace good workers than to invest in them. So many leaders are floundering and don't know what it takes to be great; instead, they're promoted because of who they know, not based on their capability or skill set.
- 77 percent of businesses report that leadership is lacking.[1]
- Uninspiring leaders only drive 23 percent engagement within their teams.[2]
- Only 33 percent of employees report feeling engaged.[3]
- 69 percent of employees say they would work harder if they felt their efforts were better recognized.[4]

- Close to 50 percent of managers don't trust their own leaders to do the right thing.[5]
- Where authenticity is encouraged, employee production increases by 20 percent.[6]

A tremendous gap exists in our workplace, and it's the lack of authenticity in leaders. Authentic leadership enhances the organization's performance and elevates employee engagement and satisfaction levels. Authentic people are self-aware, bring 110 percent to the table, and exude honesty and integrity, earning the respect and loyalty of others. How do we support each other to develop our authentic leadership style and be the best we can be as leaders? There's a great need for trusted leadership advisors and accountability partners.

This book is designed to encourage and support leaders as they seek for their authenticity. A leadership advisor partners with leaders, teams, and the entire organization to achieve their goals and objectives, supporting them as they strive to reach their full potential. An accountability partner is often a trusted friend or acquaintance who checks in on a regular basis and supports you in keeping your commitment to your goals.

The journey to being an authentic leader is not an easy climb and doesn't necessarily take the simplest trail; it may take many different paths. Once a leader has reached the mountain apex, very few are standing with them. Those who aspire to be authentic typically have support and respect from their various teams along the climb, but not always from their counterparts. To be more authentic is to be intentional daily and to know and stay true to who we are as we recognize our imperfections and continuously improve. We are always young enough to learn and better ourselves. This practical guide will help start conversations in building the skill set in the up-and-coming generations of leaders, seasoned leaders, and all those in between.

~~~~~~

"Great leaders are not the best at everything. They find people who are best at different things and get them all on the same team."[7] —*Eileen Bistrisky, Effective Leadership Consulting*

~~~~~~

CHARACTERISTICS OF AN AUTHENTIC LEADER

What is your identity as a leader? Do you know how others perceive you and what your reputation is? Are you comfortable with who you are? Do you know your leadership style? To be an authentic leader, you need to know what that means and how you will be that type of leader. There is no cookie-cutter formula, but it does require a skill set that's not prevalent in today's business world and actually goes against the grain. You need to know confidently who you are and what you represent. To be authentic is not typically accepted or rewarded in our society, so we tend to adapt to what's expected and accepted in business. Authentic leaders will garner trust, relate to their teams, and inspire and challenge them while being open to new ideas and solutions.

"Before you can become an authentic leader, you have to know who you are. That's your true north: your most deeply held beliefs, your values, the principles you lead by, and what inspires you."[1]
—Bill George, Author of *True North: Emerging Leader Edition*

1 LEADERSHIP

Key Insights

- An authentic leader will create a legacy of inspiring, challenging, and encouraging growth in your team to become and do more than they thought was possible.
- Leadership should be viewed as an honour and privilege, not a right. Be confident in who you are and your capabilities.
- Look at the big picture and get your team to look at it occasionally to help them remember why they're doing what they're doing.
- The goal of a leader is not to serve themselves at the expense of others. They allow others to take credit when things go well and take responsibility and reflect on their actions when things go wrong.
- When we stop taking or needing credit, we can help others succeed and progress.

Guidance

- What are some common leadership styles? What is your style?
  - Transformational—inspiring and innovative, constantly improving the organization, which builds and maintains employee satisfaction. They aren't always good at making quick decisions or problem-solving.
  - Delegative—fully trusts the team and doesn't manage or provide direction, especially when course redirection is needed. They tend to take away value from the organization versus adding value.
  - Authoritative—good when quick decisions need to be made but can come across as a dictator and are not respected if they take a "my way or the highway" approach.

- o Transactional—will reward those who have achieved expectations, but they don't deal well with change and are not innovative, as they don't think outside the box.
- o Democratic—collaborative by including their team in everything, listening to their opinions and ideas to get buy-in. However, this can create an environment of groupthink, where decisions can't be made and there are endless meetings.
- o Strategic—a visionary who coordinates growth, creating respect and inspiration. They can fail to communicate the vision clearly and fixate on it, blocking other ideas.
- o Servant—develops the people who follow, will put people first, and are generous with high employee engagement and morale. They tend to focus on the people and not the organization's goals.

- What does leadership mean? What does it mean to you?
  - o Have a vision of the future and communicate it to the team.
  - o Maintain focus and direction for your team while reducing/eliminating roadblocks and distractions.
  - o Guide changes and continual improvements to sustain success. Be a decision-maker. Stay calm in stressful situations.
  - o Fight for your team—be their most prominent advocate.
  - o Do not be afraid to ask for help and guidance.
  - o Manage the risks—ask people what is keeping them up at night.
  - o Be proactive instead of reactive.
  - o Keep your word and deliver. Communicate openly and honestly.
  - o Build relationships with your team and the business. Be adaptable to people and situations.

- What makes a good leader?
  - o Define their reality (i.e., family stresses, marriage trouble, broken relationship, division on your team, and victimization that left you traumatized).
  - o Possess resilience and endurance to deal with challenging situations that continue and are not solved in a short amount of time.

o Recognize the different leadership styles and switch between them depending on the situation.
- Do you ever compromise your true self in your leadership style?
- What constrains you or is in your way of being a great leader?

Reflection

- Think of the leaders you have worked with and are currently working with. What are their leadership styles?
  o What do you appreciate or dislike about their styles?
  o What changes do you need to make to your style to be like the leaders you appreciate?
- Evaluate and document your current reality with your family, your marriage, your job, and your career.

2 AUTHENTIC SELF

Key Insights

- Self-awareness is how we perceive ourselves through our experiences, thoughts, emotions, feelings and physical self. As we become more emotionally aware, we can help prevent how we react and reduce false beliefs.
- Perception—If this is healthy, you'll take on more challenges and achieve your goals.
- Thoughts—Be mindful of your thoughts. If they're negative, try to improve your thought processes. Over time, they will change and become more positive.
- Emotions—We have various emotional states, and recognizing and accepting them will help our relationships professionally and personally. Emotions come before feelings and are experienced subconsciously or consciously. They are a reaction and the raw data prior to feelings being involved.
- Feelings—We must identify and determine which ones are associated with our thoughts and emotions. Feelings are experienced consciously, generated through our thoughts, and can be more biased and altered.
- Physical—Our bodies tell us how situations/words impact us and are usually expressed through facial expressions, heart rate, voice, or other ways. We need to be aware of this, as this is a very public response.

"From the experience of the past we derive instructive lessons for the future."[1] —*John Quincy Adams, Former United States of America President*

Guidance

- What does it mean to be your authentic self?
    - o This ensures that our actions match our words and are true to our beliefs and values.
- What strategies can you use to help find your authentic self?
    - o Do a self-inventory—discover and evaluate how you respond to various situations and challenges. Do you stay true to your core values and beliefs or put on a mask?
    - o Be present—try to block out the noise and chatter in your head and focus on what's in front of you now.
    - o Evaluate day-to-day actions—your daily actions and interactions make up your authentic self. Evaluate internal and external motivations and distractions.
    - o Communicate boundaries—give yourself permission to say no. Assertively communicate your needs to help in preventing unhealthy situations.
- Questions for a self-inventory:
    - o Perception
        - How do you perceive yourself?
        - What can you do to make your self-perception more positive?
        - How do you know what other people think without them telling you?
        - Are you putting on a negative filter based on your perception and not the other individual's?
    - o Thoughts and Emotions
        - What are your thought processes?
        - How do they impact your emotions?
        - How can you change those thoughts and emotions to be more positive?
    - o Feelings
        - How do you feel about yourself?
        - What are your feelings when others are talking about you?

- ▪ What feelings are connected to your thoughts and emotions?
  - o Physically
    - ▪ How do you physically respond to emotions (i.e., facial expressions, body movement or something else)?

Reflection

- Take time to process and document your experiences, thoughts, emotions, feelings, and physical responses throughout your day. Is there a pattern emerging?
- Ask for feedback on different situations to gain a different perspective. This is humbling and builds your character.

3 PLAYING TO YOUR STRENGTHS

Key Insights

- As a leader, wanting your team to be successful is one of the greatest gifts you can give to them.
- Using the strengths we've been given drives our passion and enthusiasm. We become more driven and focused on growing and developing.
- There needs to be a balance of focusing on our strengths and weaknesses.

"He who believes is strong; he who doubts is weak. Strong convictions precede great actions."[1]
— *James Freeman Clarke, American Theologian*

- Once you discover who you are in your strengths, you can choose how to use those strengths in your career going forward.
- An authentic leader needs to know when to play to their strengths and when it will be a disadvantage (i.e., evaluate the company's culture).
- Self-awareness is key in understanding your strengths and weaknesses, as it will help build your emotional intelligence.
- Uniqueness in your leadership role involves knowing your weaknesses alongside your strengths and managing/balancing them effectively.

Guidance

- How can a leader identify their strengths?
  - o   Do a self-assessment. There are many on the market.
  - o   Ask for feedback from trusted sources and your team.

- o Understand what motivates your team and what their strengths and weakness are. They can help you be better at skills they excel at.
- o Continue to focus on developing and growing these strengths.
- How can a leader develop their identified strengths?
  - o Know and understand your leadership style's strengths and weaknesses.
  - o Get a leadership advisor or accountability partner.
  - o Expand your network to create opportunities to observe other authentic leaders in action.
  - o Target specific skills that you want to improve on and set a plan in place to monitor progress of improvement.
  - o Practise what is learned from research and feedback.
- What are your strengths? What are you naturally good at?
- What are your differentiators?
- When you analyze your tendencies, you'll start to see a pattern and be able to adjust accordingly. This will support you in developing the areas of strengths and weaknesses you may need to work on. Evaluate your behaviours/tendencies in situations such as:
  - o Dealing with stress.
  - o Dealing with difficult people.
  - o When your ideas are ignored.
  - o When you find something difficult to do or feel like you don't have the knowledge to do it.
  - o When you've been successful.
  - o When you've been shown respect.
- How would you redesign your job so that you can better play to your strengths?
- Are there elements of your character that have the potential to be strengths if you worked on them? Stretch yourself to form new strengths.

Reflection

- Make a list of areas you consistently get positive feedback on.
- Write a description of who you are at your best.
- Identify the best leaders you've worked with and what skills made them the best.

4 RECOGNIZING YOUR WEAKNESSES

Key Insights

- Recognize and understand your weaknesses.
- Weaknesses are not deterrents but opportunities.
- No matter how much you improve or gain experience from your weaknesses, you will always have them. It's the awareness and growth that are going to support you in becoming an authentic leader.
- No one is perfect, so don't aim for or become obsessed with perfection.
- Acknowledge your weaknesses and be vulnerable. We're all human and make mistakes. No one is perfect!
- Leading is about connecting with your team; one of the best ways to do that is to acknowledge your weaknesses.
- Admitting you have weaknesses does not mean you're weak. It's a strength.
- Don't be afraid to ask for help or support.

Guidance

- Why is it valuable for a leader to recognize their weaknesses?
  - o It's extremely humbling and difficult to be honest and admit our weaknesses, but in the long run, it's required to become a more well-rounded leader.
  - o Allows a leader to target the weaknesses to improve on.
  - o Creates a reliance on others to fill the gaps, producing a team that complements each other while building others up to understand their value.

- How can a leader identify their weaknesses?
  - o Do a personal reflection and inventory on strengths and weaknesses.
  - o Ask peers and team members for insights into potential weaknesses and improvement recommendations.
  - o Review past performance reviews.
  - o Use assessment tools.
- How can a leader work on their weaknesses?
  - o Once weaknesses have been identified, create a strategy to improve them.
  - o Make the changes required and regularly review and adjust the plan.
  - o Seek feedback from the team and other leaders as you improve on your weaknesses.
- Some common leadership weaknesses and what to do about them.
  - o Inability to make decisions—Work with a leadership advisor to support you in making clear and objective decisions.
  - o Micromanagement—Delegate projects/tasks and allow the team to do them their way. Provide guidance upon request. Trust your team!
  - o Poor communication verbally and nonverbally—Clearly and concisely communicate what is needed/required and in a timely manner. Take time to be present and actively listen and watch body language.
  - o Unable to empower others—Get to know your team and their skill levels; put them in charge of their own work and be there for support and guidance if required.
  - o Inadequacy of self-awareness and emotional intelligence—Learn to read the verbal and nonverbal communication as well as take responsibility for your actions.
  - o Failure to be adaptable and accept change—"My way or the highway"—Listen to feedback and act on it to stay adaptive and innovative.
  - o Lack of empathy—Try and view things from other people's perspectives.

o   No direction or vision for the team—Establish a vision with goals so the team can work together to achieve them.

o   Insufficient ability to deal with conflict or give constructive feedback—Provide timely, concise, clear, respectful, and encouraging feedback as soon as possible after a situation has happened.

o   Focus on being liked—There needs to be a balance of being liked and doing the job.

Reflection

- Make a list of areas in which you consistently get feedback on your weaknesses. Share with your leadership advisor or accountability partner to support you in working through these areas.

5 EXPECTATIONS FOR YOURSELF· DO THEY NEED TO BE ADJUSTED?

Key Insights

- Practise grace. Maintain a sense of respect and care for yourself and your team even when it doesn't seem deserved.
- Expectation setting never ends!
- Gratitude is necessary. We have so much to be thankful for each day. Look for "joy moments" throughout your day. Some days are more challenging, but there's always a "joy moment" in each day, such as a kind word, someone making you laugh or smile, or you bringing a smile to someone's face.
- Sometimes we need to say it's good enough and not aim for perfection. Perfectionism reduces our ability to prioritize. Focus on leveraging the Pareto Principle 80/20 rule, which helps us manage our time more effectively. The Pareto Principle holds that 80 percent of the results will come from just 20 percent of the effort. When doing something, we need to get to a point where 80 percent is good enough, as the last 20 percent takes 80 percent of our time to complete.

Guidance

- How does one set realistic expectations for themselves?
    - o Determine your values and what's important to you.
    - o Identify your goals and break them down into achievable tasks.
    - o Set achievable timelines for your goals.
    - o Be adaptable. Adjust your expectations when things don't go according to plan.

- o Know your boundaries and limits.
- o Stop comparing yourself to others. This is your story and journey.
- o Mistakes will be made, but don't let fear of failure stop progress. Give yourself grace.
- What are your expectations of yourself as a leader? At work? At home?
- Are your expectations realistic? Are they within your control?
  - o Why or why not?
  - o Do you need to adjust your expectations of yourself?
- What are some actions you can take to reset expectations? What actions are you going to take to adjust expectations of yourself?
  - o Determine what your expectations are for yourself.
  - o Learn to let it go—If we don't let things go, we can become negative and tend to beat ourselves up. Stop it! You're likely achieving more than others, but you just don't see it. Perfectionists struggles with letting go. It's okay to be human, make mistakes, and fail, as that's where growth happens.
  - o Practise positive self-talk—Remind yourself of all the positive comments and feedback you've received. Keep a book or a wall of stickies to encourage you when self-doubt and negative talk creep in. Review all your accomplishments and what you have done great.
  - o Give yourself grace! This is a hard one, as we so often beat ourselves up. But if you take a step back and realize that a little more time would be beneficial to meet the goal, then do it. We need to have realistic expectations, which involves having flexibility. Being rigid doesn't help when there is change.
  - o Be thankful for what you have and don't always look to what everyone else has. Stop comparing but be authentic and accepting of who you are. We have so much to be thankful for, and it may help to take your eyes off yourself and go and help someone else in need to readjust your gratitude.

o   Do not give up! You may need to keep trying and readjusting your expectations of yourself.

o   Make sure that you choose healthy expectations and ones that are attainable and realistic.

Reflection

- Evaluate and document:
  - o What are some achievable expectations for yourself?
  - o What are you thankful for?
  - o How can you practise being grateful?
  - o How are you going to give yourself grace in the future?
  - o How will you stop the self-negative talk and create positive feedback for yourself?

6   LIFE PRIORITIES

Key Insights

- Knowing your priorities is important, as it will increase your confidence and you'll spend time in areas that mean the most to you. If your priorities aren't in alignment, you'll experience increased stress, unhappiness, and a sense of being unfulfilled.
- Priorities are only a few things that you put above other things.
- Goals are desired results to achieve one's objective.
- Be intentional/purposeful.
- Remove the distractions.
- When a crisis happens, we become very aware of our priorities and remove what's less important. We need to prioritize when things are calm, as there will be less room for regrets.
- By setting our priorities, we stop doing things that aren't important to us.
- Know that your priorities can change over time.
- We tend to be "busy" but often with things/activities that don't support our priorities and are in our comfort zone. Get comfortable with the word "No," as you'll be saying "Yes" to what truly matters to you.
- Knowing what your life priorities are will help in directing your day-to-day tasks and focus. It will allow you to say yes or no to achieve your goals.
- Priorities help you to set boundaries.

Guidance

- How does a leader identify and set their priorities?
  o Define their values, what they stand for, and what they believe in.
  o Intentionally evaluate and determine realistically what they can achieve each day and which matches their goals and values.
  o Don't commit to saying yes before they evaluate if it's a good fit or not.
  o Make small changes over time to align their values and priorities.
  o Regularly check in with themself and their leadership advisor or accountability partner to reflect on and adjust areas to meet their values and priorities.
  o Determine what distracts them from achieving their priorities, (i.e., technology, television, or "being busy").
- What happens if leaders aren't clear on their priorities?
  o Constantly reactive instead of proactive, as they are dealing with urgent, in the moment situations.
  o Unable to make confident and quick decisions.
  o Base priorities on other people's versus defining their own.
  o Cannot meet their commitments, as they believe they can do it all.
- Do you know your priorities (i.e., faith, family, friends, work/career)?
  o What are they?
  o Do they need to be adjusted?
- What are your values?
  o You will know what matters once you determine your values by reflecting on your life.
  o You will have confidence and clarity in making choices that align with your values.

Reflection

- Take time to reflect and be honest with yourself about your priorities. What is your vision for your life?
- What are you going to do to be intentional with your priorities?
- Lay out a plan of action to help you maintain your focus and direction.

7 BOUNDARIES

Key Insights

- Boundaries force us to take ownership and responsibility for ourselves.
- Part of our identity is in the workplace, and we need to take responsibility for our work and set clear limits.
- If someone on your team fails to do their job, find out the root cause, as they may be passing the buck instead of doing the job themselves.

> *"Effective workers do two things: they strive to do excellent work, and they spend their time on the most important things. Many people do excellent work but allow themselves to get sidetracked by unimportant things; they may do unimportant things very well!"*[1]
> —Dr. Henry Cloud & Dr. John Townsend, Authors

- Boundaries are an ongoing battle and may need to be adjusted for different situations. As you stick to them and see positive outcomes, you'll become more confident in who you are.

Guidance

- What are common workplace issues? How to set boundaries for each of them:
  o Taking on other people's responsibilities.
    - Talk to the individual who is giving you their work and let them know you will not be able to help them out.
    - When asked to do something that's not part of your job, say no and hold to that boundary, despite their reaction.

- Do not try to justify why you won't help.
- Do all of this calmly. Don't fight anger with anger.
- Bailing out a responsible co-worker is okay if it doesn't become a habit.

o Working too much overtime.
- Decide how much overtime you're willing to do.
- Review your roles and responsibilities description.
- Outline your weekly and monthly tasks.
- Discuss with your boss.

o Priorities need to be appropriately managed.
- Set a budget for the time you have each week. This will force you to select essential items.
- Select excellent versus good tasks; you want to maximize your time.
- Work smarter and you'll be amazed at what you accomplish.

o Difficult coworkers.
- You can't change anyone else but yourself. When you believe you can change someone, you lose power and control.
- The only response you can own is yours. When you realize this, you can change how you respond to your coworker and regain control over yourself.
- Be cordial to these individuals who are complex and critical, but distance yourself, as you don't want to be wrapped up in their world.
- If you have strong reactions to someone, evaluate why. Ask yourself probing questions to get to the root cause, as something from the past can trigger it.

o Workplace Drama
- Manage your expectations and ensure that you separate personal from business. There will be times when these lines cross, but only sometimes. Work is not obligated to provide emotional support for your issues or hurts.
- Deal with your work issues directly and get to the root cause so that they don't impact your personal life.

- Part of identity is your job, so make sure you understand your gifts and talents and set clear boundaries, as this will impact your happiness overall. Do not let others define who you are.
- What are your boundaries regarding work?
- In what areas do you need set boundaries?
- How are you going to start making the necessary changes in setting boundaries?

Reflection

- Over the next week and month, document areas where you have set boundaries. Identify where you need to set boundaries. Also note how people respond to those boundaries, as they may initially struggle or may embrace them.

8 STRESS, WORRY, AND CONTROL

Key Insights

- Take care of yourself.
- Control means moving forward with your vision and goals, knowing that change is inevitable. It's being present, focused, and intentional, removing distractions and the need to be reactive.
- Understand what you have control over and what you do not.
- We can't worry about what we have no control over. Worry is a form of arrogance, as you think you're the only one who can deal with the situation.
- We must face our stress/worry, which isn't easy. It will take us down and make us ineffective if we don't deal with it.
- View dealing with stress and worry as an opportunity to show your strengths and develop creative ideas to solve the situation.

Guidance

- How do you respond to stress/worry?
- What can a leader do to reduce stress/worry?
    - o Acknowledge their emotions and pinpoint what exactly is causing the stress.
    - o Breathe, take a step back, put things in perspective, and evaluate the situation and how to respond.
    - o Slow down. Take a break, walk away, and come back to it.
    - o Prioritize and plan out their time.
    - o Learn to say no.
    - o Review the track record of their successes.
    - o Talk to an encouraging friend or colleague.

- What are some areas in your business that could cause stress/ worry?
  - o It can be any number of different things:
    - Unreasonable employee or boss.
    - Having to make major decisions quickly.
    - Presenting to the senior management.
    - Unexpected issues.
    - Challenging team members.
- What is your worry based on, reality or emotional assumptions?
  - o Do you have control? If no, dismiss it.
  - o Are you confident that it will go wrong? If not, ignore it.
  - o Is it unknown? If yes, dismiss it.
  - o The more you remove emotional thoughts, the less you will have to worry or stress about.
- What are some areas you have control over within your business unit that could cause stress?
  - o You have control over how you respond to various situations; you cannot control how others respond.
- What areas do you have no control over within your business unit/team?
- Is it acceptable for a leader to put their team under stress?
  - o Yes, remember, there is a balance. A leader wants to challenge and motivate the team to achieve their full potential.
  - o If one does not put sufficient demand on the team, they won't perform well.
  - o More pressure with little support, and they will underperform.
- How does a leader know if they are putting the right amount of pressure on the team?
  - o Assess the current state, watching for those who are too comfortable, those who are in panic mode, or those who have entirely withdrawn.
  - o Ask them! Don't just observe it.
  - o Provide coaching and pointed feedback.
    - Add or remove the structure to the problem.
    - Provide encouraging and positive feedback.

- Break the problem up into smaller pieces.
- Show your team by your actions and words that you have confidence that everything will work out.

o Resist the urge to fix poor performance, allowing the individual to fail. If a leader fixes it, they enable poor behaviour instead of allowing the individual to change and improve.

o Once a leader understands the stress levels, they can turn up or down the heat.

Reflection

- List what can you do that's in your control to reduce your stress with family and job.
- Make a list of what you can do differently in dealing with stress on your team and how you can involve your team in reducing the stress.

9 DEALING WITH HURT

Key Insights

- In life, we all hurt or irritate someone or are hurt or irritated by others. We are all porcupines to someone.
- We need to forgive and learn to live in peace with everyone. That doesn't mean we forget or hold grudges. Grudges not only hurt us but those around us.
- Abusive relationships are not safe to continue. We have control over the hurt, feelings, and responses of those abusers.
- We cannot control what other people say about us or how they hurt us, but we can control how we respond to those who hurt us and what we say about them.
- Hatred, resentment, and unforgiveness will cause you to live in bondage and negative fallout in relationships with others. They also impact your mental health and your ability to move forward.
- When someone lashes out at you, try to understand what's happening, as they are likely hurting. Don't excuse the behaviour, but try to understand what's behind the anger. Listen to them to discover what's occurring and help them find a way through their pain.
- Don't let hurt divide your family or team. Don't repay people with evil for evil. As a leader, you need to rise above your human nature and seek to address the hurt maturely. This sometimes means seeking professional help or stepping away from the situation to regain focus and process how to deal with it.
- Revenge is only sometimes seen. It can be silent or behind the scenes. Don't be sneaky or underhanded, recruiting allies

behind the scenes to undermine someone's life and leadership, or slandering someone's character or influence. Let it go!

- The world longs for forgiveness.

"Forgiveness is a virtue of the brave."[1]
—*Indira Gandhi, Former Prime Minister of India*

Guidance

- What does a leader need to do when someone hurts them or feels hurt by them?
    o Do not stew, brew, or talk to everyone else about how awful the person is. This is slander.
    o Go to them in private.
    o Seek an understanding of others' feelings and viewpoints.
    o Provide insight into your side of the hurt with respect and gentleness. Be kind and gracious to them.
    o Be willing/humble enough to apologize.
    o Even if they don't ask for forgiveness, forgive them. This will do more for you and your mental health than you realize, and it goes against everything society tells us about how to respond. This will involve surrendering your ego and pride and how you react to those who hurt you.
- How do you know when you've released/forgiven the ones who have hurt you?
    o It doesn't hurt anymore; you no longer see them as enemies and won't feel uncomfortable in their presence. It doesn't mean you'll be close friends with them.
- What does forgiveness do for your life and work?
    o Can you imagine someone not forgiving you? Where would we all be if we couldn't start over?
    o Forgiveness breaks the chain of pain and revenge.
    o Forgiveness will let them off your hook and remove them from having rental space in your life. It's a choice; you will be free from bitterness and resentment. Resentment will eat

away at you and stop you from functioning in the present and the future. This a process and not easy to do.

o   It doesn't settle questions of blame, justice, or fairness.

o   It does allow for relationships to start over. Some relationships may not restart once we have forgiven. That's okay. Give yourself permission to let go and move on, as there is a need to recognize that some relationships are only for a season and are not healthy to continue.

•   How do you typically deal with hurt? What can you change in your process of dealing with hurt?

Reflection

•   Write down if there is hurt in your life you need to deal with and forgive. What is it? What steps are you going to take to resolve it peacefully?

•   List how can you help your team with their hurts and frustrations.

10 PASSION

Key Insights

- When you are fulfilling a need with your talents and abilities, you will become passionate.
- We are drawn to individuals who have found their passion because they inspire us with their enthusiasm.
- We can waste away in self-indulgence or find our passion and joy and, in doing so, encourage others to do the same.
- Passionate leaders put aside their agendas and genuinely listen to understand.
- Passionate leaders inspire others to achieve the organization's vision, goals, and direction. There is a drive to work harder, a desire to grow and succeed, and a determination to push through the struggles. You and the team will learn what it truly takes to be successful.
- A leader needs to be passionate, because if not, the team won't be either. There will not be growth, the ability to push through struggles, the desire to show up to work, or the ability to care.

Guidance

- Why is it important for leaders to find their passion? How do leaders find their passion?
  - o If they see a gap and feel the need to fill that gap, they have likely found their passion.
  - o They may only have some skills to fill the gap, but when they find their passion, they'll develop and grow those skills.
  - o They take risks and step out of their comfort zone, ignoring the fear of failure.
  - o They seek advice, research options, and test it out.

- How can a leader encourage their team to find their passion?
    - o Being passionate!
    - o Knowing and understand their team and what motivates them.
    - o Allowing people to do their jobs and not micromanaging.
    - o Encouraging growth through coaching and training.
    - o Creating a positive environment.
- What are you passionate about?
- Are you currently doing what you're passionate about in your career?
    - o If not, do you need to re-evaluate what you're doing as a career?
    - o How are you going to find out what you are passionate about?

Reflection

- Start having honest and real conversations with yourself and others if you're not passionate about what you're doing in your career and life. Make a plan to investigate and identify what you are passionate about and how you're going to achieve it. Have your leadership advisor or accountability partner support and guide you in obtaining your goal.

11 CONTENTMENT

Key Insights

- Contentment is a long-lasting feeling of being satisfied and at peace with your circumstances and who you are. It's a state of mind that requires continual practice as it accepts the situation in life and works to improve it. A person continues achieving and excelling to reach their goals and dreams.
- Content leaders use their skills, delegating to their team to develop their strengths while remaining focused on the end goal.
- It is being fully present, participating in the moment, and using your knowledge and resources to deal with whatever comes your way.
- Contentment for leaders is often overlooked and undervalued, but it's a new level of leadership potential.

Guidance

- What is the difference between happiness and contentment?
  - o Happiness is a short-term feeling that comes with fun, laughter, and excitement.
  - o Contentment is a long-term feeling of satisfaction and fulfillment, which comes with inner peace and the ability to maintain a positive attitude.
- What are some ways to find contentment?
  - o Know who you are and stay true to yourself. Do not compare yourself to others.
  - o Surround yourself with people who will encourage, motivate, and support you.
  - o Act on your goals and priorities.

- o Take care of yourself. Sometimes you must put yourself first over anyone else to ensure your cup is full to give back.
- o Let go of the hurts and anger from the past. Don't allow them to define you negatively. You have the ability and responsibility to move forward, using those experiences to impact and support those around you positively.
- o Find the "joy moments" in each day you are grateful for. Show people your appreciation.
- o Be present in the moment and the activity, removing all the clutter and noise in your mind. Turn off your technology.
- o Celebrate ALL accomplishments.
- o Choose to be content, as it is a choice!
- What are some benefits of contentment for yourself?
  - o Less stress and anxiety are experienced as you focus on what is truly important to you.
  - o Healthier and stronger relationships are developed, as you can communicate your needs better.
  - o The need for more things is removed, as you're thankful for what you have, and you don't have voids to fill.
  - o There is a tendency to stop comparing and being jealous of others.
  - o You can trust yourself and others easier.
- How does the team benefit when you're content?
  - o Your attitude influences the team and the work environment.
  - o It changes how you interact with the team, and you build meaningful relationships.
  - o There is a greater appreciation of the team and their accomplishments.
  - o You become the calm in the storm when facing challenges and make thoughtful choices and decisions.
  - o There is less stress, as you are prone to being proactive versus reactive, which means less worry and negativity.
  - o You inspire growth and learning.

Reflection

- Determine what areas you need to work on in being content and document how you're going to work on those areas.
- Identify and reach out to the champions that will encourage and motivate you.

LEADERSHIP TRAITS TO BE AUTHENTIC

We can all be good leaders, but what traits make us authentic leaders? What do we need to do to achieve them? These characteristics are not highly regarded in our society, yet they set great leaders apart from the rest. These are rarely found in managers, as they take incredible work and go against what has become acceptable.

> *"Authentic Leaders are not afraid to show emotion and vulnerability as they share in the challenges with their team. Developing a solid foundation of trust with open and honest communication is critical to authentic leadership."*[1] *—Farshad Asl, Author of* <u>*The "No Excuses" Mindset: A Life of Purpose, Passion, and Clarity*</u>

12 HUMILITY

Key Insights

- Critical factors required to turn good companies into great ones need steely determination and an attitude of humility.
- Humility is a misunderstood characteristic and is thought of as negative or weak. It's actually a positive characteristic and is developed through experience.
- Low self-esteem means you lack self-confidence or self-worth. This is not to be confused with humility.
- When recognition is our motive for doing something, this is pride, which is a negative virtue. Pride seeks more and more beyond control.
- Pride means seeing yourself as more than what you are. It can also mean viewing yourself as less than what you are.
- A humble leader can be more authentic, as they know their strengths and weaknesses and bring a sense of compassion to their leadership style. They don't require or seek out recognition and are not doormats.

Guidance

- What is the difference between humility and humiliation?
    - o A humiliated person feels helpless, hopeless, weak, enslaved, powerless, dishonoured, and torn down.
    - o A humble person feels helpful, hopeful, empowered, willing and strong to help others, dignified, builds up.
    - o Humiliation is a tragedy; humility is a choice.
    - o True humility is a rare trait and is challenging. It takes effort and has great rewards.
- How do we develop humility?

o   Recognize our pride—Be honest with ourselves and admit we have a problem with pride. Don't think of yourself more or less highly than you ought to. Pride is what destroys!

o   Quietly serve others—When we serve others, we take our eyes off ourselves and see things through others' perspectives.

o   Keep listening and learning—Don't assume you have all the answers and that you're always right; be willing to hear what others have to say.

o   Hang out with ordinary people—Society is all about the extraordinary, not the ordinary.

   ▪   How do you rank people in your circle—by wealth, looks, status, or what they can do for you?

   ▪   Are you obsessed with your status?

o   Stop taking yourself seriously—If you can laugh at yourself, it helps to make you human and approachable. If you're so wrapped up in your pride you're busy caring about the perceived image and you can't laugh at yourself.

o   Don't lose perspective—Take time to enjoy your natural surroundings, such as your city and the surrounding areas, the mountains in their grandeur, the vastness of the land, or the stars in the night sky. When we look at these, we become so small in the scheme of things, and so do our troubles.

•   How can you show humility to your team?

Reflection

•   Who in your circle keeps you grounded against pride? Talk to them about holding you accountable.

•   Figure out how you can quietly serve, where you will not get public accolades.

13 INTEGRITY

Key Insights

- Truth-teller ability reveals your level of integrity.
- Say what you mean and mean what you say.
- Be true to who you are. If people can't value the true you, find people who will.
- Integrity is sincerity, which means being truthful and genuine. You are who you are in all situations.

"Always do right. It will gratify some people and astonish the rest."[1] —*Mark Twain, Author*

- Authentic leaders don't hide behind a mask. What you see is what you get, with no agenda.
- The greatest compliment is someone recognizing your integrity.
- Actions have significantly more impact and speak louder than words. Words are cheap if the actions don't match. Our actions MUST match our words!

Guidance

- What is integrity vs. honesty?
    - o Honesty allows others to be able to trust us and recognize our dependability.
    - o Integrity is a strong moral compass that adheres to high ethics and standards. You will do the right thing even when it's difficult, or when no one is looking, and at any cost.
    - o Honesty can happen without integrity, but integrity does not happen without honesty.
- How much integrity do you have?

- o Do you justify your actions when you know you are wrong?
- o Are you checking and evaluating your motives?
- o Are you excusing yourself?
- Who are you?
  - o What are you like with your family and children? With your spouse?
  - o What are you like at work with leaders above you? With your team? With counterparts?
  - o What are you like under pressure?
- Do your actions match your words?
  - o If your actions match your words, the benefits are overwhelming:
    - It is critical and required for being a leader.
    - The team/individual will know you will support them and have their back implicitly. They will do the same in return.
    - There is a new level of trust and respect garnered and a deeper willingness to follow you as a leader.
    - You can respect yourself and stay true to your authentic self.
  - o If our actions do not match our words, there are consequences to the misalignment:
    - The team/individual will lose respect and trust. They will look at you and wonder if it's worth being part of your team.
    - It's demotivating and uninspiring.
    - It disrespects the individual/team and devalues their abilities and contributions. They know when you are being ingenuine.
    - It also minimizes you and who you are truly meant to be.
- With whom do you associate? Are they the individuals who will make you better or tear you down for their gain?
  - o These individuals will influence your behaviours. You need to surround yourself with people who will support and challenge you to be the best version of yourself.

"People of integrity don't abandon their values and principles under pressure. They know that times of adversity and temptation are precisely when values and principles matter most. They keep promises. They fulfill obligations. They maintain their honour even when it is costly to do so."[2]
—Pat Williams, Author

- How can you demonstrate honesty and integrity at work?
  o Speak the truth in a way that will not create more conflict. Think before you speak!
  o Acknowledge your mistakes.
  o Respect others' thoughts and opinions.
  o Recognize others' success.
  o Be the example your team should follow.
  o Do not compromise your morals or your authentic self.

Reflection

- Do a moral inventory of yourself, hold yourself accountable by documenting it, and start confronting yourself truthfully.
- Evaluate who you are in all your relationships.
- Find someone who can hold you accountable to be an individual of integrity.

14 VULNERABILITY

Key Insights

- Vulnerability is perceived as a weakness when it's actually a strength that endears you to your team.
- Authentic leaders are vulnerable and will gain the trust of their team quickly, as they are willing to share their struggles and connect at a deeper level.
- When a leader is willing to admit their mistakes, it drives the courage to be innovative and builds trust amongst the team. When a leader pretends to be perfect and expects perfection from the team, they create an environment in which the team avoids admitting they made mistakes and the risk of making them.
- Vulnerability does not come naturally but takes a lot of hard work. We need to let go of who we think we should be and be intentional about this.

"A leader, first and foremost, is a human. Only when we have the strength to show our vulnerability can we truly lead."[1] —Simon Sinek, Author and Speaker

Guidance

- What is vulnerability?
  - o Risking the exposure of emotions, uncertainty, taking risks and being okay with it.
  - o Taking ownership for something that went wrong (i.e. at work, in relationships).
  - o Asking for feedback on strengths and weaknesses from your team.

- o There still needs to be boundaries by not talking to everyone about others or being completely open. There is a balance of professionalism when dealing with your team. You do not need to tell everyone you meet your life story.
- What is the power of vulnerability as a leader?
  - o Creates an environment of authenticity, collaboration, open communication, and trust.
  - o Improves innovation, engagement, and success.
  - o Makes you more approachable as a leader, especially when mistakes are made. The team tends to admit to them versus covering them up or avoiding them.
  - o Able to navigate difficult situations with greater ease and build stronger, more meaningful connections due to understanding your own emotions and others.
- How can you be more vulnerable as a leader?
  - o Be authentic—Be true to yourself instead of who you think people believe you should be. There's no need for perfection, and you'll be seen as a visionary versus a dictator.
  - o Admit and own your mistakes—This will create an environment in which your team will feel safe and comfortable to do the same.
  - o Actively listen—To build trust, people need to feel that they are being heard and can share their concerns and secrets. A micromanager will be unable to gain trust with their team.
  - o Embrace discomfort—It's not easy to be vulnerable, so take baby steps to be more accepting of it. This may involve asking for feedback and being open and honest about your mistakes. Look at this as an opportunity for growth and self-awareness.
  - o Allow others to shine in their strengths—You won't have all the answers, but when you allow your team members' strengths to excel, it shows that you are secure as a leader and your team is not a threat to your leadership.
- Does your organization allow for a culture of vulnerability?
- What changes can you make on your team to create an environment of vulnerability?

Reflection

- Questions to ask yourself and document your answers to better understand where and why you struggle with vulnerability.
    o What are you afraid of losing by being vulnerable?
    o What are you trying to prove that hinders you from being vulnerable?
    o What are you trying to hide that is stopping you from being vulnerable?
- What steps can you take to improve vulnerability in yourself and your team? Write them out.
- Start implementing these changes and take note of the changes within the team.

15 SELF-DISCIPLINE

Key Insights

- Every aspect of your life, including your thought life, emotions, behaviours, and actions, is impacted by your ability to be self-disciplined.
- Self-discipline is something you embrace enthusiastically, as it will change your life.
- Successful people practise self-discipline a lot!
- It requires commitment through your actions and the support of people holding you accountable.
- This journey is your own and cannot be compared to the journey of others.
- Our maturity and growth are dependent on our ability for self-discipline.
- We will only want to change and become self-disciplined once we become dissatisfied with how things are.
- There will be days when you feel like you're pushing a boulder up a mountain; continue to move forward, not yielding to your human nature, as you will be rewarded. You will become strong and will not live with regrets.

Guidance

- What does a self-disciplined life look like for individuals working on this trait?
    o More satisfaction with their lives, as they are better at avoiding temptation.
    o Live more in the present and embrace each moment.
    o Compete against themselves to continue to challenge themselves.
    o Recognize they could be better and continue to strive for their goals.
    o Continue to improve as they practise.
    o Know how to set boundaries. People around them may try and sabotage them as they change, so they will change who they surround themselves with to achieve their goals.
    o Enjoy life more and do more of what they genuinely want, even pushing themselves out of their comfort zones.
- How do you start to build and change habits?
    o Identify the change/habit you want to make and break it into smaller pieces.
    o Do one small change repetitively until it becomes a habit.
    o Add another small change and then another until the significant change becomes routine.
- What is an area/habit you would like to create and work on?
- How are you going to start to build self-discipline in this area?

Reflection

- Identify someone or a couple of people who will hold you accountable to achieve your goals. Choose people who will support you and not try to sabotage your journey. If they do, eliminate them from the accountability role. There will be people who will try to discourage you on your journey due to jealousy and insecurities.
- Start working on achieving your goal in small changes and be aware of the behaviours that come with it, good or bad, and adjust accordingly.

16 ENDURANCE

Key Insights

- Life isn't easy, including our careers, and endurance is needed. It's not a want but a need, as it requires fortitude and perseverance to withstand adversity. To be authentic, there is a demand for endurance in: unyielding moral compass, physical stamina, self-awareness, and emotional intelligence.
- Endurance is a marathon, not a sprint. We must embrace our adversity, which pushes us to persevere and, in turn, builds our character.
- Be all right with ambiguity, as it builds endurance and resilience. Ambiguity forces us to be responsive to the in-the-moment realities we face and supports us in bouncing back. It tends to result in a more objective approach to last-minute changes or events, which always happens in leadership and life.
- You must maintain your sense of confidence.
- Believe in yourself and your ability to see things through to the end.
- Find your passion; it will make enduring much more manageable than fighting against the tides of things you don't enjoy. The road may be challenging, but being passionate will make it worthwhile.
- Quitting is not an option! You won't respect yourself if you do.
- Keep achieving; this is where you can lose your passion.
- Leadership is not a role but an endurance activity.

Guidance

- What are some strategies to build endurance as a leader?
  - o Get comfortable with ambiguity. There will always be change and disruption, but what's important is how a leader develops their communication and change-management abilities. A leader will be okay to say, "I don't know the answer, but I'll find out." This is a perfectly acceptable answer—just don't use it as a crutch for everything.
  - o Persevere through it all. A leader requires emotional intelligence, an unyielding moral compass, and physical stamina, especially when facing defeat. They need to dig deep to find the strength to stand up, dust off, and move forward.
  - o Encourage collaboration. Leaders and teams are having to do more with less. Teams that collaborate effectively are able to come up with innovative and creative solutions by bringing in different perspectives and viewpoints.
- What is required of a resilient leader?
  - o Taking control of the situation.
  - o Making solid decisions based on facts and current information under pressure.
  - o Motivating and encouraging the team.
  - o Excising mental toughness and having the determination and fortitude to keep moving ahead.
- What are the benefits of endurance for a leader?
  - o Improved respect and loyalty from the team.
  - o Increased productivity and innovation.
  - o Enhanced confidence in decision-making abilities.
  - o Boosted collaboration amongst the team and overall performance.
- How do you deal with challenging situations that require persistence and endurance?
- What is holding you back from achieving what you would like to do?
  - o Are you willing to remove the roadblock?

o   What is stopping you from removing it?
- Are you thinking of quitting?
  o   What do you think will happen if you do?
  o   Are you going to have regrets?
  o   If you do quit, are you prepared to tell your family and friends and see and hear their responses?
    - Are you prepared to deal with how they think of you in the future?
    - What do you think their response will be?

Reflection

- Endurance can be a lonely place as a leader and it requires support. Evaluate who is in your circle of champions and whether they are right and will support you when dealing with difficult situations. If some need to be replaced, consider who you should attract to be in your corner. Be honest and truthful with yourself.

17 COMPASSION

Key Insights

- Compassion is something you show by doing. It's what you do and how you do it to influence and inspire others to do the same positively. It doesn't weigh the cost but responds with kindness.
- Sometimes we need to sit in the mud puddle and listen instead of getting a stick to pull people out.
- We all have been shown compassion.
- Compassion comes at a cost. The cost can be one or a combination of possessions, time, money, and priorities.
- It can be difficult to show compassion when emotionally fatigued because of the perceived cost. Awareness of our stress, responses, and priorities is key. We need to ensure our "cup" is not empty and take time to tend to ourselves in order to care for others.

Guidance

- Why is compassion necessary in leadership?
  - o Creates strong connections between people.
  - o Increases trust and loyalty.
  - o Encourages enriched collaboration.
  - o Presents the leader as more competent.
- What are some challenging situations that require compassion and wisdom?
  - o Disappointing people when making difficult decisions, such as layoffs. It would be best to look rationally at what suits the business and how to be compassionate to those impacted.
  - o Having to push the agenda to get it done. This shouldn't be the typical stance of a leader. If you do have to move

the agenda forward, make sure to analyze the agendas and arguments of others, get support and buy-in, and get it done.

- o Providing challenging feedback and guidance despite not being easy to hear, such as in performance reviews. Being honest and providing constructive feedback enables the individual to understand expectations clearly.
- How does a leader show compassion to others?
  - o Start by showing themselves compassion and stopping the negative self-talk, criticizing, and demeaning of themselves.
  - o Putting themselves in other people's shoes and figuring out how to best support them. We can look at people, but when we truly see them, compassion will begin.
  - o Being human in dealing with awkward situations.
  - o Unless they act, they cannot show compassion. An authentic leader needs to use their head and heart to influence and inspire positively.
  - o Compassion is bold; it is not analytical, and it can surprise.
- What can you do to change how you view people and start to see them for who they truly are?
- When have you been shown compassion?
- When have you shown compassion to someone?

Reflection

- What tangible actions can you perform to show compassion? Start actioning these activities and analyze the responses you experience.
- What is holding you back that must be removed to show genuine compassion? Identify the steps you're going to take to develop and show compassion.

18 GENEROSITY

Key Insights

- Generosity means giving freely without the expectation of getting anything in return.
- A generous mindset leads to a more passionate leader who is interested and freely gives their time and knowledge to others.
- This is not a discipline/characteristic that comes naturally but one that can be taught. Generosity is something we purposefully and knowingly perform.
- To not give and only receive is belittling to ourselves and takes away from others receiving what we must provide—a genuinely selfish and egocentric act.
- In North America, we are some of the wealthiest individuals and have an opportunity to be generous with our time and money.
- When being generous, we may give hope to those who need it and can change the world in small and big ways. We don't know the ripple effect that comes from being generous. This is a good thing, as we would have big egos.

Guidance

- What are some qualities of a generous leader?
  - o Treats others with respect as they give the benefit of the doubt.
  - o Is patient and courteous. Does not worry about time and effort.
  - o No expectations of getting something in return and does the job before anyone asks.
  - o They tend to provide positive feedback versus negative.
  - o Is present in the here and now and is their authentic self.

- o Seeks to understand first and then react.
- Why is generosity so hard to show?
  - o We are fearful that whenever we give time, money, or energy, there won't be any leftovers for ourselves.
  - o We believe that what we can give needs to be better and more valuable.
- What can leaders do to be more generous?
  - o Start with small things that could be more important.
  - o Be spontaneous with their generosity. Do random acts of kindness.
  - o Offer their skills to help someone on the team or on another team.
  - o Turn off the TV, phone, and devices to make the time to go and be generous.
- What can be learned from being generous?
  - o Not only will others benefit, but you'll also learn more about yourself, opening yourself up to other opportunities and experiences and discovering what you are genuinely passionate about.
  - o You will become more present in daily activities, which will be impactful at home and work, as there is deeper communication and connection. This leads to more significant influence and trust with all those around you.
  - o When we naturally give of ourselves, there's a powerful motivating factor that creates growth in ourselves and strengthens lasting connections and relationships.
  - o It has a more significant impact on how your team interacts and supports each other. The message is that we care and help each other in any way we can.

Reflection

- In what areas could you improve on your generosity? What steps are you going to take to make these improvements?
- How can you help your team be more generous?

19 DISCERNMENT MIXED WITH KNOWLEDGE

Key Insights

- Every story has two sides, and one may be weaker than the other.
- Educate yourself on both sides.
- There is no single source that knows all the truth.
- If one expert says that a specific interpretation is correct, it doesn't mean it is so. Question it and see if other experts agree.
- Be objective!
- There is no course to learn discernment; it can happen if you let it.
- Don't believe everything you hear. Check it out, put it to the test, mull it over, and think it out.
- Get multiple perspectives.
- It's good to question what you're being told, but there's a fine line between discernment and suspicion. Learn self-restraint and be teachable.
- Discernment creates self-awareness, while knowledge alone creates arrogance.

Guidance

- What's the difference between knowledge and discernment?
  - o Knowledge involves acquiring facts, experiences, and principles.
  - o Discernment involves intuition/gut instinct, reading between the lines, a sense of truth and good, sizing up a situation or person.

- o Discernment acknowledges that my knowledge is limited and I need others.
- What are the benefits of discernment and knowledge?
  - o Knowing the information and understanding will help you critically determine the best solution for the business, people, or a situation.
  - o You'll become more perceptive of people and environments by building understanding from observing and reflecting. This, in turn, creates deepening insights into various situations and relationships.
- How does a leader gain a balance of discernment and knowledge?
  - o Look at the big picture.
  - o See multiple viewpoints.
  - o Be tolerant.
  - o Value opinions, even ones with which you disagree.
  - o Acknowledge that you don't know everything and can learn more.
  - o Be forgiving and gracious.
  - o Be teachable and open to the counsel of others.
  - o Learn from experiences and the people before you.
- What is your standard approach to dealing with different situations?
- What situations and decisions do you currently face that require you to use discernment and knowledge? How are you going to handle them?
- Which way do you lean when dealing with a problem: knowledge or discernment?

Reflection

- Evaluate and document a current situation in which you could change your approach to be more balanced. What steps are you going to take?
- Share with your accountability partner how you're going to mix discernment and knowledge going forward. Document the changes you have seen in the last week, month, and year.

20 CONSISTENCY

Key Insights

- A consistent leader says what they mean and means what they say. This builds trust and increases the ability to influence the team.
- A consistent leader has defined their values and purpose. This will inspire others and help align your team.
- Treat others equally, no matter the circumstance. Be fair and avoid favouritism.

Guidance

- Why does consistency matter?
  - A leader who is consistent with their approach makes it easier for the team to work with and predict responses/behaviours.
  - It builds trust and morale in the team.
  - If the leader is inconsistent, the team will follow the same approach.
  - Goals will be achieved, as consistency drives focus and actions.
- What does inconsistency breed?
  - Fear, as the team doesn't know how or what your response will be.
  - An environment of inaction and indecisiveness.
  - A workplace of ebbs and flows with no real direction and the foundation constantly changing.
- What is a consistent leader?
  - Has a defined purpose and values.
  - Takes ownership of their success.

- o Sets measurable goals.
- o Focuses on what is in their control.
- o Ensures they take care of themselves mentally and physically (self-care).
- o Inspires and supports others to be successful.
- o Endures adversity.
- o Understands the difference between determination and stubbornness.
- o Behaves consistently, no matter the situation, even if they don't feel like it. They don't let their mood or behaviours change from the normal, consistent ones.
- Are you a consistent leader? What areas do you need to improve on?
- How can you be a consistent leader?
  - o Understand your core values and make decisions based on those.
  - o Communicate your values to your team.
  - o Demonstrate your values, even if it's uncomfortable.
  - o Find and commit to your style, making everyone aware so that your team knows what to expect. It doesn't mean having the same manner as everyone else.
  - o Admit when you've been inconsistent and why. This will help to continue to build trust in your team.
  - o Ask your team to hold you accountable for inconsistency, and allow for discussion and questions.

Reflection

- Define and document your core values and purpose as a leader. Take the time to reflect and determine who your authentic self is.
- Do you compromise on your values to get what you want and to achieve what needs to be done? Document where you are compromising and the changes you need to make.
- Take time to evaluate where you can make improvements in being consistent as a leader and on your team.

21 REPUTATION, SIGNIFICANCE, LEGACY, AND TALENTS

Key Insights

- How you treat people and make them feel, and how successful of a leader you are, will define your reputation in the industry. Do not burn bridges; always do your best and be the best version of yourself.
- Reputations are based on what people believe to be true about: your characteristics, personality, and values at work and outside of work, and who you surround yourself with. Actions speak louder than words when it comes to reputation.
- Reputations take years to build and can be lost in a moment when abuse of power and privileges happens.
- Our reputations precede us whether we like it or not. This can create demand and growth in our careers, or negativity and take longer to grow.
- Stop seeing yourself as the centre of the universe. The trend is to be self-centred, focusing on oneself and your happiness, advancing oneself, and being right. Do not conform to this way of thinking and living.
- Do not think more highly of yourself than you should, as you are only one person who requires others to be successful.
- Pride can reveal itself in two ways as the focus is on us:
  o When we think too highly of ourselves (our abilities, accomplishments, when we think we can do everything, or when we believe that what we do is more important than what others do).

- o When we think too little of ourselves (too little of our talents or what we contribute) and believe we aren't worthy or qualified to do something.
- We need to stop viewing ourselves with self-righteous pride. We need to accept what we can and cannot do.
- We must embrace the truth regarding our inabilities and stop comparing ourselves to others, wishing we had their abilities and talents. We need to focus on the talents we do have and use those skills to encourage others.

Guidance

- How does a leader discover their reputation?
    - o Do a 360-degree evaluation by asking their boss, counterparts, and their team for an honest assessment.
    - o Do their own self-evaluation by evaluating their strengths, weaknesses, skill sets, and the people they surround themselves with personally and professionally.
    - o Compare the 360-degree and personal evaluation to determine if they align and if there are any changes that need to be made.
- How does a leader build their reputation?
    - o Define their leadership value and proposition along with any unique differentiators.
    - o Be mindful of who they align themselves with. They surround themselves with individuals who will positively challenge, encourage, guide, and hold them accountable.
    - o Understand their strengths and build on them.
    - o Figure out what is holding them back and let it go.
    - o Know and trust their authentic selves, be more transparent, acknowledge when they make mistakes and be smart enough to reach out for help.
    - o Be aware that perfection is unachievable, fake, and makes them come across as unapproachable. Leadership is a learning journey full of trials and errors, which makes a leader approachable and respected.

- o Be purposeful in reflecting weekly on how they're doing on developing a positive reputation.
- What type of reputation do you have currently?
- o What would you like your reputation to be in the future?
- o How will you achieve it?
- We all have a deep desire for significance, but at what cost?
- o Is it self-centred and a prideful significance, or one that will be truly impactful and different from today's trend?
- What are your talents and abilities?
- o How can you use those talents on your team?
- o What are the talents of your team?
- How do your team's talents complement your abilities?
- o We all have different talents and abilities that can be used to make an effective team.
- o Some talents are more significant and prominent, while others are less obvious, but all are important.
- o When you ignore or cut off people and their abilities to meet the team's needs, you minimize and marginalize these individuals. These individuals lose their purpose and motivation.

Reflection

- Evaluate and define your talents, strengths, and weaknesses.
- Evaluate your team's talents and determine how they can fill in for your weaknesses and benefit the team.

22 SELF-AWARENESS

Key Insights

- Self-awareness involves understanding our emotions, skills, and personalities. The more we comprehend ourselves and our reactions, the more we can recognize and understand these traits in others.

> *"Today, in the hybrid world of work, self-awareness is even more important. That's because human connection is waning while building relationships based on trust and honesty is becoming harder as real-world interaction between and a leader and her people (and among team members) is diminished."*[1]
> —William Arruda, Senior Contributor, *Forbes*

- Self-awareness is essential in authentic leadership, as these individuals know their values and who they are. Their actions match their words, which increases trust in the team, allows for positive responses and reactions to difficult situations, and improves communication.
- It allows you to be thoughtful to your team and provide support before they ask.
- You can control your response to situations and be the voice of reason and the calm in the storm.
- Self-awareness isn't a common trait in leadership, yet it will impact a company's bottom line.
- Stock performance was tracked over 30 months, from July 2010 through January 2013. During that period, the companies with the greater percentage of self-aware employees consistently outperformed those with a lower percentage.[2]

- In a study of 17,000 individuals worldwide, the Hay Group Research found that 19 percent of women executives interviewed exhibited self-awareness as compared to 4 percent of their male counterparts.[3]

Guidance

- What are some of the benefits of self-awareness?
  - o Able to connect and build up your team, creating an effective and collaborative team.
  - o Able to put yourself in other people's shoes, which in turn builds stronger relationships and creates a positive work environment.
  - o Understanding of your communication style and the impacts on the team.
  - o Better conflict management resolution.
  - o Ability to understand peak performance times and manage your time effectively, increasing productivity.
  - o Knowing when to take on new challenges to grow yourself.
  - o Finding purpose and meaning in your work, providing greater job satisfaction.
- How can a leader grow their self-awareness?
  - o Understand their strengths and weaknesses.
  - o Set boundaries and stick to them.
  - o Know what triggers their emotions.
  - o Seek out feedback and be willing to apologize when necessary.
  - o Find ways to stay focused and improve productivity.
  - o Lose the need to be number one. Don't be self-seeking but be willing to learn about other people.
- How can you assess your behaviours and responses?
  - o Assess your patterns and behaviours. Ask yourself five times "Why?" to get to the root cause.
    - Be careful not to analyze your responses continually, as this can tear you down. This exercise should be done to better understand your reactions to different situations and not become an obsession.

o Understand what your triggers are, as these will change as you grow and improve yourself.

o Learn how to be yourself with more skills. This can be done by determining when it will be advantageous to use your personality traits and when to put certain ones aside.

o Ask for feedback from trusted sources to identify your blind spots.

- How self-aware are you? How do you respond in different situations such as:

  o A team member missing their timelines and not communicating it prior to the due date? Or slacking off so that others have to step in?

  o Being told you must do this project despite you sharing all the proven risks of absolute failure? Once the project fails?

  o People coming to a meeting with a set agenda and bringing new items/topics to the table?

Reflection

- Think about and document what can you work on to start to improve your self-awareness. Where do you need support/ accountability to achieve better self-awareness?

- Reflect on a situation in which you reacted negatively and ask yourself "Why?" five times to determine why you reacted the way you did. This will create self-awareness of yourself and your response to various situations.

23 TRUTH-TELLING

Key Insights

- Truth increases trustworthiness, credibility, reliability, influence, and respect.
- Truth is a sign of having the best interest of those around you in hand and having a solid moral compass.
- Telling the truth takes courage, as it can be unpopular. There will be backlash, but stay strong and hold on to the truth.
- Understand the audience and their potential responses.
- A lie hurts more than the truth. A lie will always come out, and the truth will free you.
- Being truthful is becoming an anomaly.
- Today, people have their "own truth" that can change daily, but the truth is meant to be forever.
- If a leader is unable to be honest and truthful, then they should not be in leadership. Honesty means not telling lies, while being truthful means sharing all the facts and a realistic account of the situation. You can be honest without presenting the full truth of the matter.

Guidance

- Why is truth-telling so crucial an authentic leader?
  - o They stay true to who they are.
  - o They have a clear conscience and look at themselves in the mirror.
  - o They do not have to remember what they said. When you lie, you must retain all the lies, which is stressful.

- o They find courage and bravery that they didn't have before.
- o They inspire others, and they earn a level of respect.
- o They will have deeper relationships and connections.
- Why is truth-telling so vital for the team?
  - o It allows us to grow as leaders and learn from our mistakes, setting an example of expectations for our teams.
  - o It creates an environment of open and honest communication within the team.
  - o When issues arise, the team can feel valued and work together to resolve the problem.
  - o Respect, trust, credibility, and reliability become the leader's reputation.
  - o Self-interest is set aside when telling the truth.
  - o It creates a cohesive team who will look out for each other and not fear retribution for speaking the truth.
  - o Individuals who are divisive and liars will be removed or leave, as it's uncomfortable and they can't control various situations.
- What happens when truth-telling is not happening on a team?
  - o There is infighting, power struggles, and sabotage within the team.
  - o The undermining of the leader and company initiatives reduces the performance of staff and the overall organization.
  - o Creates a toxic environment with confusion and anxiety.
- How does an authentic leader build relationships so that people can speak the truth?
  - o Understand and know their audience. When starting on a team, they must build those relationships and determine how to best present information.
  - o Tell the truth no matter what. Be very cognizant of how they deliver the message. This can be gentle, factual, and, in some cases, blunt—dependent on the relationship and situation. Self-awareness is key!

Reflection

- What situations could have had a different outcome had you spoken the truth?
- Is there a current situation in which you need to speak the truth, and what approach will you take?

INSPIRING DYNAMIC TEAMS

How do you create a dynamic team as a leader? How do you inspire a team to be the best they can be? Trust is a core characteristic and value every team needs. This can quickly be built through you as a leader by being consistent in your messaging and actions. You must invest in your team by getting to know and develop them as individuals. Create a positive environment and address issues quickly and effectively. Your leadership and example will guide and direct the team. As the team works together, learns to appreciate all that everyone has to offer, and challenges each other, the team will become a well-run machine of success.

"Leaders instill in their people a hope for success and a belief in themselves. Positive leaders empower people to accomplish their goals." —Unknown

24 CREATING A POSITIVE ENVIRONMENT

Key Insights

- If you are being negative ... STOP IT! This is counterproductive and destroys teams.
- Treat people with honour and respect.
- By not caring who gets credit, you can enjoy yourself and will be able to do so much more. You'll be free to focus on others to encourage and build them up.

"Life is 10 percent what happens to me and 90 percent how I react to it."[1] —Charles Swindoll, Pastor and Author

- Our attitude drives our situations and outcomes and is far more important than anything else.
- When you are struggling, take your focus off yourself and go and do something for someone else (i.e., take someone out for coffee, encourage someone, help someone in need). There are days when you will need more energy or strength to do it.

Guidance

- How does a leader create a positive environment?
    o Encourages open communication and collaboration.
    o Creates growth strategies for employees.
    o Acknowledges mistakes and is approachable, providing guidance as required.
    o Promotes diversity and inclusion.
    o Manages by walking around each day, knows all the names of their team, and learns something about everyone.

- o   Models the behaviour they would like to see from their team.
- o   Supports fun and socialization.
- What are the benefits of fostering a positive environment?
  - o   Increases productivity.
  - o   Reduces turnover.
  - o   Improves employee engagement.
- Are there situations on your team that need to be addressed immediately?
  - o   Suppose you are dealing with a situation in which someone spreads negative gossip, looks for dirt, and is constantly negative. In that case, you need to hate this behaviour, confront it, and deal with it immediately in a caring and firm way, as such behaviour impacts your team in huge ways by dividing and destroying them.
- How are you going to address those situations to change the dynamics?
- Are you the issue on the team and creating negativity? What can you do differently?
  - o   Find your passion, which may mean re-evaluating your career choice.
- What is your attitude like as a leader?
- What changes do you need to make to improve the environment?
  - o   Get out of the way and allow your team to do their jobs their way. Do not micromanage.
  - o   Support, coach, and mentor your team.
  - o   Push people to leave their comfort zones and think outside the box.
  - o   Create an environment that allows people to make mistakes, fail, and learn from them.

Reflection

- Do a reality check of yourself and how you impact your team negatively and positively.
- Document what changes you need to make and how you're going to achieve them. Evaluate in a week and in month if you're making the positive improvements.

25 THE VALUE OF KNOWING YOUR PEOPLE

Key Insights

- Understanding the goals and objectives of those working with you.
- Knowledge of each employee's value adds to and effectively leverages their skill sets.
- Leads to employee satisfaction, empowerment, and success as a leader.
- Authentic leaders ask the right questions of people.
- Show your team that you value and respect them by celebrating their successes and engaging them in consultations, where you listen to them.

Guidance

- Why is it important for a leader to know their team?
  - o They will build trust and respect.
  - o They will be able to understand their behaviours and motivators.
  - o There will be openness and comfort in freely approaching them in any situation.
  - o They can create environments that will work with each employee, such as a collaborative (extraversion) or a quiet one (introversion).
  - o There will be an increase in productivity and empowerment of the team.
- Do you know your team?
  - o Do you know the full name of each member of your team?

o Do you know something personal about each one? What is their story?

o What motivates the individuals on your team?

o Do you know each team member's strengths and what they can bring to the team overall?

o Do you know their weaknesses and how to support them?

o Are you utilizing their skill set fully?

o What do your employees value (i.e., career, good work, money, family)?

- What can a leader do to show they know their employees better?

o One-on-ones. You will find out a lot, as there will be more freedom to share what's happening with them personally and professionally.

o Be compassionate about what is happening in their lives but don't allow their hardships to produce mediocre work.

o Understand the skill set of people working with you and encouraging development. Your team is only as strong as the weakest link.

o Team building activities outside of the work environment or less professional gatherings, such as breakfast or lunch, will allow you to get to know your team on a different level.

o Show and tell your team that you have their backs in various situations, as long as it's not unethical.

Reflection

- Get to know each one of your team members' stories and what motivates them.
- Start having one-on-ones with your team to determine their skill set and how to use them more effectively.
- How will you show your team that you value and need them? (i.e., Bring in breakfast or treats, check in on them as you walk by their cubicle/office, and say THANK YOU!)

26 MOTIVATING PEOPLE AND TEAM BUILDING

Key Insights

- Invest in your team and make sure you understand their worth.
- Not retaining staff is costly. Everyone is replaceable, but at what cost? Recruitment of a new hire is costly, as there is the need to recruit and train and a loss of productivity. They also need to gain the knowledge of the employee who leaves.

> *"Many studies show that the total cost of losing an employee can range from tens of thousands of dollars to 1.5–2X annual salary."*[1] —Josh Bersin

- Humble yourself and follow your staff individually to see their daily tasks. It will give you a greater sense of the heartbeat of your organization and what is and is not working.

Guidance

- What are some of the benefits of motivating a team?
  o Productivity increases with appropriate motivation.
  o Reduced turnover, as there is job satisfaction and engagement.
  o Increased innovation and creativity.
- How can a leader motivate their team?
  o Share the vision and goals and consistently communicate.
  o Understand the organization's culture.
  o Encourage collaboration and teamwork.
  o Provide positive feedback and encouragement and reward them.

o Offer development opportunities and give your team room to thrive.

o Create a healthy and safe team environment where they can have honest conversations and you are approachable.

o Get to know your team by determining their needs, which will help you understand what motivates them. We all need stability, opportunities for growth, and a chance to contribute.

o Prioritize your team's wellbeing by asking about them and their families.

o Adapt to changes in doing business (i.e., working remotely, hybrid, or in the office).

o Support your team by doing mundane tasks so they can work on the more complex work to meet timelines and succeed, especially if they are responsible workers. If they tend to be lazy, delegate their work to others, or procrastinate, this may be an opportunity to allow them to fail to learn the lesson.

o Follow your team members for a day to gain insight into what they do and where improvements and changes can be made.

o Ask your team for help, especially in areas you are weak in.

o Trust your team!

o Fight for your team and have their backs.

• What are some practical things a leader can do to motivate the team?

o Put a three- to-four-week look-ahead on a wall of all the tasks on stickies. Each person has their colour of stickies with their tasks and realistic timelines for the week in which the job will be completed. Then at the daily stand-up or weekly status meeting, review the tasks to ensure everyone is on track. If the tasks continually move to the following weeks, you can quickly see who is struggling and ask what you, as a team, could do to support them. It creates competition, and individuals want to avoid being highlighted as falling behind.

o   Stay late with the team, bring them food, walk around, and ask them how they are doing.

o   Arrange team building activities outside the office, such as bowling, arcades, go-carts, or mini golf.

o   Bring in lunch, breakfast, or treats to team meetings.

o   Make bets with the team for various treats/prizes; for instance if the team is behind on their tasks, challenge them to complete those and their current ones within a week or two. If they can catch up, buy them all lunch. No one wants to be the person who caused everyone to lose out on their free lunch.

o   Set the tone using "we" versus "I" or "me."

o   Go for coffee and get to know each person on the team.

o   Understand what motivates them and how to meet their needs.

o   Show sincere appreciation for the work that's being done.

Reflection

•   Identify what do you need to work on to be more effective at motivating your team.

•   Do something to motivate your team and bring back insights that you got out of it. Don't show the team once and expect things to change immediately. You'll have to do this multiple times.

27 BUILDING TRUST IN YOUR TEAM

Key Insights

- The basic needs that teams need to be met are trust, compassion/empathy, stability, and hope.
- Support and encourage. If one fails, we all fail, but if one is successful, we all are successful.
- Be fair and encourage open, honest communication.
- Be transparent. The more transparency, the more trust will increase.
- Help people achieve their goals. Allow your team room to grow, and be there when they fall/fail.
- Keep your promises and follow through. This will show you are committed and that your team can depend on you. Broken promises can lead to disillusionment and trust being ruptured.
- Be humble. Share your experiences with failure and success.
- Avoid micro-managing.

Guidance

- What is the value of trust?
  - o You are setting the stage for the culture and how the team will function and behave.
  - o When people trust their leader, they will show up and do their best work.
  - o It increases productivity, creativity, and results.
  - o People are doing more with less and need to know their leader will support them and have their backs.
- How does a leader build trust on their team?

- o Provide a clear set of expectations of how the team needs to work and function.
- o Jointly create with your team a vision, mission, and values that also support the corporate vision, mission, and values.
- o Get to know your team and care about them.
- o Encourage your team and praise them for a job well done.
- o Use people's strengths effectively.
- o Delegate tasks completely, even if it's easier to do the tasks yourself. Consider inviting team members to facilitate weekly team meetings or represent you in various meetings.
- o Allow people to do their jobs the way they want as long you get the required outcome.
- o Figure out what motivates everyone.
- o Empower people to implement new ideas and solutions.
- o Allow your team to make mistakes and support them in working through them.
- o Be approachable and friendly, creating an open-door policy.
- o Ensure your words and actions match consistently.
- o Model the behaviour you want from your team.
- What are some struggles in building trust?
  - o Balancing the external business realities and the internal people realities. For example, there is a need or urgency for business or process changes and recognizing people's mindsets and behaviours to meet those changes.
  - o Knowing the personalities, responses, and styles of work methods of each member of the team and allowing for those differences.
  - o Understand if you are the type of leader that trusts the team immediately or if you expect the team to prove themselves before trusting them. Both can work. The individual who trusts firsts and allows the team to prove otherwise will be able to build the team's comradery faster.
  - o Trust is easy to lose and hard to win. It impacts our professional and personal reputations and credibility.

- What areas do you need help in to trust your team? What must you change?

Reflection

- What areas must you improve in to build trust within your team and organization?
- What can you do this week to show your team you trust them?

28 BUILDING TRUST WITH YOUR STAKEHOLDERS

Key Insights

- Figure out win/win solutions. This involves researching and understanding your stakeholders, investing in them, and actively listening to them.
- Understand where trust has been broken and where the pain points are to avoid making the same mistakes.
- Practise open, honest communication with clear expectations of what you can do for them.
- Communicate when you have made a mistake, taking responsibility for it.
- When you make a commitment, follow through on it.
- Be proactive, showing that you're taking responsibility for your area and that your stakeholders can count on you.
- Do not go with a "sky is falling" mentality but with one that sees a problem with potential solutions. This will show your thoughtfulness and innovation to the problem.
- The benefits of building trust with stakeholders are that it speeds up decision making and problem-solving, reduces uncertainty, and increases confidence. There will be tremendous respect for you and your abilities.

Guidance

- What can leaders do to learn and invest in stakeholders?
  - o Research the stakeholders and past engagement experiences.
  - o Understand their expectations.

o   Provide honest and realistic expectations of what you as a leader will be able to provide for them and the process.

o   Follow through on commitments.

o   Acknowledge mistakes and communicate them with the stakeholders.

- How can leaders build better relationships with their stakeholders?

o   Get to know who they are and understand their needs.

o   Help where you can without asking for anything in return.

o   Provide clear, concise, and regular communication.

o   Provide potential solutions to problems.

o   Provide reasons behind decisions.

o   Try to understand where they are coming from and their perspective.

o   Avoid the word "but."

o   Continually demonstrate your capabilities and competencies.

- Are you pessimistic, or do you find ways to seek out the positive?

o   What can you do to be more proactive and positive if you are negative?

- In what areas and situations could you improve in asking for help?

- Do you tend to own your mistakes or pass the buck?

o   People find it harder to yell at someone or be upset when the person has taken full responsibility. It takes the wind out of their sails and increases their respect.

Reflection

- Take time to identify situations in which you can improve building trust with your stakeholders.

- Practise coming up with solutions to problems that include outside-the-box thinking. This may involve a meeting with your team to get their insights and ideas.

29 THE REALITY OF OFFICE POLITICS

Key Insights

"Office politics is the activities, attitudes, or behaviours that are used to get or keep power or an advantage within a business or company."[1] —Merriam-Webster Dictionary

- Refrain from differentiating between your leaders and team members.
- What you do for one, you must do for the other. Treat everyone equally.
- Value the success of the team versus the individual.
- Respect your employees for them to respect you.
- How you handle office politics will determine how you are viewed and it will impact your career.
- Do not stick your head in the sand; avoid negative office politics. You must play the game but know how to play it with integrity.

Guidance

- What are the types of political organizations?
  o Minimally political companies—Standards for promotions and expectations for managing and leading are made clear, and underhanded forms of politics are avoided.
  o Moderately political organizations—Political behaviour, where it does exist, is low-key or deniable.
  o Highly political arena—Formally sanctioned rules are only invoked when convenient to those with power. This is an environment of who you know, not what you know.

- How can a leader influence or create office politics through their actions?
  - o They can play politics and do it ethically. Present the facts and persuade people to their side; do not use rumors or misinformation.
  - o Recognize that when dealing with people, there will always be politics, but what matters is whether it will be negative or positive.
  - o Politics will impact a leader's performance and career.
    - Build relationships, or you will miss out on opportunities and could lose your job.
    - Do NOT suck up/butt kiss to build relationships.
    - Summarize what you have done, how it has impacted the organization, and why it is essential.
  - o Try to remain neutral during conflicts. Sometimes this is impossible and ineffective; you must take a stand while staying true to your core values.
  - o When something is "taken offline," or chatting before a formal meeting, is still political as you try to influence and engage to be more effective.
  - o Being politically savvy takes effort and requires focus, practice, and being intentional. Do NOT sell out your authentic self to get ahead, as you will not respect yourself or others.
- What steps can a leader take to manage the politics within their organization?
  - o Employees get involved in negative politics when bored, unmotivated, and unchallenged.
  - o Be the positive change you want to see in office politics by:
    - Being impartial.
    - Creating job satisfaction.
    - Being transparent at all levels.
    - Defining cultural values for the department. (Review your company's values and determine if they match the principles and ethics you want for your employees.)

- Communication, communication, communication involves actively listening so that the individuals feel heard (need to use multiple methods, such as written, verbal, and nonverbal).
- Would you want to be your co-worker? If not, what can you do to gain respect and inspire others?

Reflection

- Review your company's values and determine if they match the principles and ethics you want for your employees.
- Define the cultural values you want your department to have. Once these are defined, you as a leader must live up to them along with the team.

COMMUNICATION

There are many ways to communicate; even in our silence, we speak volumes. Sometimes we need to be comfortable in our silence to force others to participate in the communication. Our body language, facial expressions, and tone of voice are all part of our communication. What and how topics are written will also determine the outcome. We must be aware of our verbal, physical, and written communications, as this significantly affects the desired results.

"If you can't simplify a message and communicate it compellingly,
believe me, you cannot get the masses to follow you."[1]
—*Indra Nooyi, former PepsiCo CEO*

30 COMMUNICATION

Key Insights

- How we communicate with our teams sets the stage for the type of working environment in the future.
- Drop the ego! You don't need to be the most intelligent person in the room; stop and listen to the input of others.
- Sometimes we need to take a step back from the situation and breathe. Learn to be comfortable in silence and take a break to gather your thoughts and emotions.
- Better to give bad news as quickly as possible, as there will be more options to fix it than waiting until the last minute/eleventh hour.
- Treat people how you want them to treat you. Don't surprise them, and be upfront no matter what is happening.

"Mistreating people then avoiding communication is
not 'protecting your peace', it's avoiding accountability"
—Unknown

Guidance

- What are some communication styles and their impacts on the team?
  - o Assertive—Clearly and respectfully state opinions and feelings. This is typically the most effective communication style, as many situations/problems can be dealt with rationally, proactively, and with a positive outcome. Assertive communicators are naturally confident and can

look at the picture holistically, including people's feelings, responses, and analytical aspects.

o   Passive-Aggressive—They won't deal directly with the issue but will subtly undermine the issue and person. This is a very toxic type in the workplace, as they spread discord, gossip, and negativity and should never be tolerated. To change this behaviour, one must look at the motivation and where the frustration is coming from.

o   Aggressive—The people are in it for themselves and can be verbally abusive. They won't take responsibility and want to win at all costs. This style should be avoided in most cases. Aggressive communicators are extremely difficult to work with and have significantly high team turnover. These individuals must be aware of their body language and tone of voice. They need to stop trying to win the conversation and be open to other viewpoints aside from their own.

o   Passive—These people avoid the expression of thoughts and opinions. They act as the victim and are "people-pleasers," as they're easygoing and try to avoid conflict. These individuals need to learn to say "No," not compromise on everything, and be confident in who they are and what they bring to the team.

•   What are some communication types on a team and the information they require?

o   Analytical—They need data and facts.

o   Intuitive—They want the big picture and don't want to get bogged down in the details.

o   Functional—They want all the details outlined to connect the big picture into a neat package.

o   Personal—They are concerned about everyone's feelings and want to solve the conflict peacefully.

•   What are some tips for communicating effectively?

o   Be direct and simplify the message. Refrain from inundating people with too much information.

o   Use stories to engage and draw people in and to build trust.

o   Know your audience and what information they need. Different groups need different information, so adapt accordingly.

o   Be prepared. Look at different viewpoints and have potential solutions to address any issues or concerns.

o   Read the body language of the individuals in the room and be aware of your body language and what it says.

o   Actively listen and encourage everyone to provide input and feedback.

o   Don't do it alone; involve others in developing action plans.

- What is your communication style?

o   No one is 100 percent one style. They typically have a primary and a secondary type.

- How comfortable are you in communicating with your team? If you aren't comfortable, what is causing the discomfort?

- What communication style is your team inclined to follow?

Reflection

- Define your communication style. What is the communication style of each individual on your team? What areas of improvement do you need to work on with your communication? Start adjusting to improve your skills.

31 NONVERBAL COMMUNICATION

Key Insights

- Nonverbal communication is complex, and interpreting nonverbal communication takes various abilities, such as interpersonal skills and self-awareness.
- It is communication without using words and can be unintentional and out of a person's control.
- We create clarity, trust, and rapport if nonverbal communication reinforces our words. If nonverbal communication contradicts what we verbally communicate, it sends mixed messages and can cause distrust, confusion, and hurt feelings.
- Our tone of voice will impact the response we get, and we have the power to control our response to the situation.

Guidance

- Why is nonverbal communication impactful?
  - o We do it daily, whether we realize it or not, as we can relate to, engage with, and establish relationships with those around us.
  - o How we interact with people determines how we develop those relationships.
- What are the types of nonverbal communication?
  - o eye contact
  - o body language
  - o gestures
  - o facial expressions
  - o paralinguistics (i.e., tone of voice or loudness)
  - o personal space
- How can you improve your nonverbal communication?

o Work on eye contact to show engagement. Eye contact is enormous in nonverbal communication and will tell a lot. The other aspects of nonverbal communication will support what is being said in the eyes.

o Be aware of your body language, as it matters.

o Monitor facial expressions.

o Adjust your tone of voice in various situations.

o Listen to what is being said and determine if the nonverbal communication matches. Consider potential reasons why it's not matching. Also, ask questions if it's confusing (i.e. "What I am hearing is …" "Do you mean we should …").

o Understand personal space and how different situations and cultures interpret it. Europeans are used to less space versus North Americans, who prefer distance. Standing close can be intimidating or intimate, depending on the situation.

o This is something that needs to be practised and developed.

• Reflecting on various situations, what could you have done differently with your nonverbal cues?

• What are some areas you could change and work on?

Reflection

• Evaluate meetings and different situations by looking at the following:

o What nonverbal communications did you use?

o What nonverbal communications did others use?

o What could you have done differently?

32 READING BODY LANGUAGE

Key Insights

- Body language tells a lot about a person and their thoughts. Being able to understand and read body language will set you apart.
- Your body language sets the stage for how your team and others respond.
- This skill set is continually being developed and tested if you intentionally understand and practise it.
- Professor Albert Mehrabian of the University of California created a 7-38-55 communication model, which is 7 percent communication with words, 38 percent tone and vocal, and 55 percent nonverbal in conveying feelings and attitudes. He combined the results of two studies to derive the ratio.[1,2]
- An excellent resource is *The Definitive Book of Body Language* by Allan and Barbara Pease.[3]

Guidance

- Why is body language so important to understand?
  - o It makes an impression within seconds. It determines how you will be viewed going forward, whether trustworthy, deceitful, in control, submissive, etc.
  - o Your body language needs to match your words to build trust. It will also determine if you are a leader to be followed.
  - o Face-to-face communication is the most effective and significant communication type. We interpret what people say with their tone of voice, facial expressions, and other nonverbal cues, as it provides instant feedback.
  - o You are seeing what is not being said.

- What are some nonverbal cues? This is not a definitive list but examples of what is potentially nonverbally communicated.
  o How someone sits and where they sit in a meeting states their power level. At a rectangular table, the person sitting at the end with their back facing the door is considered second in command to the person sitting at the other end as "head of the table." If you're sitting at a round table at the highest leadership level, the two individuals on either side are considered the next highest rank.
  o Types of eye contact tell you if someone is engaged, flirting, recalling information, lying, in control, etc. and need to be interpreted according to the situation and the person's behaviours. Below are examples of eye contact and meanings:
    ▪ Direct eye contact—confidence, assertiveness, sincerity, active engagement, interest.
    ▪ Averted eye contact—anxious, insecure, shy, uncomfortable, lacking of confidence.
    ▪ Avoidant eye contact—deception, guilt, shame, uncomfortable.
    ▪ Intermittent/darting eye contact—lack of engagement or interest, distracted, multitasking.
  o Handshakes are used to say who is in control, who is not, or who are equals. Below are some examples of types of handshakes:
    ▪ Equality handshake—both individuals' palms remain vertical. It shows mutual respect and equality.
    ▪ Dominant handshake—placing the palm of the hand downward when offering your hand. This is a form of aggressive communication.
    ▪ Submissive handshake—placing the palm of your hand up. This communicates that the other person has the power.
    ▪ Limp fish handshake—taken as a sign of weakness.
  o How someone uses their hands and thumbs or folds their arms shows if they are open, closed, engaged, passionate, secure, or insecure.

- o Head movements determine if we agree, disagree, are neutral, submissive, have a difference of opinion, are ready to move into action, etc.
- o Personal space. We all have our space definition, which is impacted by where we were raised (i.e., farmer versus city versus country and cultural differences). An employee coming close may want to speak confidentially; a farmer or someone who grew up in the country will extend their arm out to shake hands, creating distance, and a city individual may come closer to shake hands.
- o When lying, someone's gestures won't match their words, as they won't smile and they may touch or scratch their nose, cover their mouth, rub their eyes, scratch their neck, or tug at their ear.
- • How can you improve on reading body language?
  - o Practise reading people's body language daily and understand your body language. Watching TV and turning the sound off for periods of time is an excellent source to help practice.
  - o Understand and research what nonverbal body languages say in different situations.
  - o Understand cultural differences when communicating.
- • Times have changed, and more individuals are working from home. How can we be sure we are reading their verbal and nonverbal language, and that they are reading ours?
  - o Everyone must turn on their video cameras and look into the camera!
  - o Be aware of your body language and facial expressions.
  - o Turn off your phone and be present at the meeting.
  - o Avoid excessive movements and hand gestures.

Reflection

- • How effective are you at reading body language?
- • Be purposeful in watching people's body language and take note of yourself in your interactions for a day. Identify what you learned and what you could do differently. Do this at least monthly, if not weekly, as it will help to hone this skill.

33   WRITTEN COMMUNICATION

Key Insights

- Know your audience and their expectations.
- Be clear, concise, and factual, removing emotions.
- A well-thought-out and articulated document creates confidence in you as a leader. Effective communication creates influential leaders.
- Improving your writing skills will also enhance your analytical and reasoning skills, as you can articulate clearly and easily.
- Know when to put something in writing versus a meeting.

Guidance

- What are the benefits of writing well in the workplace?
  - o Productivity will improve, as there is very little confusion. Expectations, mission, etc. are plainly outlined.
  - o Employees are engaged and focused.
  - o There is no need to micromanage, as employees know the scope of work and their roles and responsibilities.
  - o There is less need to react and follow up on written communications, as people understand it the first time..
  - o It improves the brand of the organization and of yourself. The quality of your writing will be judged by people, whether we realize it or not. Our competency, intelligence, and integrity are all under the microscope.
- What are some techniques that can help improve one's writing?
  - o Clear, concise sentences that are not wordy or use big words when simple ones can be used and get the point across. Make ideas straightforward for the masses to understand.

o Demonstrate that you connect with everyone by understanding who your audience is. Most executives want vital points within the first two sentences of an email/letter. Some people like the fluffy, feel-good sentiments before getting into the business.

o Make complex ideas easy to understand, leaving out unimportant information.

o Read more, as this will improve your vocabulary, increase your ability to focus, and improve your emotional intelligence and empathy traits.

o Recognize that changing your written communication does not come overnight but is a process that will evolve as you practise it.

o Watch your tone in the email, as you don't want to trigger a reaction from the recipient.

• What areas do you need to improve on?

Reflection

• Identify the different writing techniques for the various leaders within your organization. How will you start adapting your writing style to meet their requirements?

34 ACTIVE LISTENING

Key Insights

- Active listening involves focusing on what the individual is saying, allowing them to finish speaking before asking questions, or echoing what you heard. Pay attention to the nonverbal and verbal cues from the speaker.
- Three types of active listening:
  - o Repeating—using the same language.
  - o Paraphrasing—using similar words and sentence structure.
  - o Reflecting—using your own words and sentence structure.
- Listen to others and seek first to understand before being understood.
- BE PRESENT! Don't think about what you'll say next, your to-do lists, or potential solutions.

Guidance

- What are some strategies to build active listening skills?
  - o Being fully present with the intent to understand the other person.
  - o Making eye contact to show that you're paying attention to the individual speaking, observing the body language and emotions.
  - o Documenting what is being said to be able to go back and review and highlight key points. It also helps to trigger points in question that need clarification after the individual is done speaking.
  - o Asking clarifying questions to ensure confusion is eliminated. It also shows interest in what the speaker has to say.

- o Remaining open minded and non-judgemental, allowing you to explore new ideas, options, perspectives, and opportunities.
  - o Summarizing what the speaker has said. If appropriate, provide your thoughts and opinions on what they have said.
- What are the benefits of active listening?
  - o Expands knowledge and understanding, improving one's emotional intelligence.
  - o Increases collaboration.
  - o Supports problem solving more efficiently, as you learn about them sooner.
  - o Shows respect and trust to the team.
  - o Encourages and motivates the individual and team, as they feel they are being heard.
  - o Builds strong relationships with the team, stakeholders, and the business.
  - o Allows you to effectively negotiate and influence.
- How does actively listening build team dynamics?
  - o The team feels heard and part of something bigger.
  - o It builds stronger relationships, as there is two-way communication.
  - o The leader becomes more approachable and likeable.
  - o There will be clearer understanding of topics, as the active listener is asking clarifying questions while reading the verbal and nonverbal cues.

Reflection

- Intentionally practise active listening throughout the week.
  - o What were the verbal and nonverbal communications from the speaker?
  - o What was the response from the individual(s) after listening to them?
  - o What insights did you learn from the topics discussed by being fully present?
  - o What could you have done differently?

35 DEALING WITH CONFLICT

Key Insights

- Open, honest communication.
- Active listening.
- Not all conflict is destructive, and it can be an opportunity.
- Know when to be silent and when to speak up.
- Deal with people and conversations as much as possible one-on-one. Be intentional about not making it public.
- Be willing to agree to disagree. We are each allowed to have our own opinions.
- Treat people how you would like to be treated, with respect and kindness.
- Fight for your team. Sometimes that means taking the fall for the team and dealing with that individual behind closed doors.

Guidance

- What are some strategies for dealing with conflict?
  - o Deal with the conflict head-on; do not ignore or avoid it.
  - o Sit down with each party, clarify the issue, and get the facts.
  - o Bring the parties together in a neutral environment, such as a meeting room, to discuss each side's perspective, actively listening to the other side and brainstorming solutions.
  - o Have the parties identify a satisfactory solution and how it will be achieved. You may have to help with this process, as you must be objective.
  - o Monitor and follow up on the situation to ensure positive progress is being made to resolve the conflict. There may still be residual tension that needs to be addressed.

- o   Know when to ask for help and bring in support to deal with the conflict.
- How does a leader deal with an underperforming team member?
  - o   Sit down with the team member and discover why they are underperforming and what can be done to improve the situation.
  - o   It's acceptable to have people removed from the project, especially if they are blatantly tearing down the team or not performing. You will gain respect from your team as you show them that you will deal with situations head-on. Also, do it quickly and do not draw it out.
- How would a leader deal with someone constantly changing the scope of work and objectives?
  - o   Sit down with the individual and determine the root cause of the issues and why they are constantly making changes.
- How would a leader deal with a project or situation where the tasks are constantly taking longer, and the project or solution is continually delayed?
  - o   Halt the project or situation, re-evaluate the objectives and estimates, and provide the client/business with realistic effort. Be transparent!
- A leader will choose their battles wisely and recognize that not all hills are worth dying on.
  - o   Are you wise about the battles you choose to fight?
  - o   Do you fight every battle?
  - o   Do you make mountains out of molehills?

Reflection

- Reflect on various situations dealing with conflict and how you could do things differently. Identify the changes you would make and purposefully adjust your response when dealing with conflict.
  - o   Recall a time when you had to work with someone difficult to get along with.
    - ▪   How/why was this person difficult?
    - ▪   How did you handle it?
    - ▪   How did the relationship progress?
    - ▪   What would you have changed?

INFLUENCING THE DIRECTION OF THE TEAM

These are not the most glamorous skills, but they make a massive difference within your team. They set the stage/foundation for how your team will move forward. They are part of a team's storming, forming, and norming stages. It will also help when new people come on board, as they will clearly understand how your team moves.

"A good leader inspires people to have confidence in the leader, a great leader inspires people to have confidence in themselves."[1]
—*Eleanor Roosevelt, Former First Lady of the United States of America*

36 EXPECTATIONS FOR YOUR TEAM·DO THEY NEED TO BE ADJUSTED?

Key Insights

- Grace means maintaining a sense of respect and care for yourself and your team, even when it doesn't seem deserved.
- Clear expectations create a solid foundation and boundaries for your team, which makes a happier one.
- Expectation setting never ends!
- Expectations are a two-way street, and both sides need to be able to communicate and question them. This also helps in empowering your team.

Guidance

- What are your expectations for your team?
- Is your team able to achieve your expectations?
- Do you need to adjust your expectations of your team?
- What can a leader do to reset expectations of a team/others?
  - o Clearly define objectives, key results, and goals and make them measurable. Establish a cadence to review objectives and goals with your team, as this will create a culture of accountability and set the team up for success.
  - o Set expectations early.
  - o Make the team accountable and empower them to achieve them. Celebrate successes, even if they are partial, to keep the team motivated.
  - o Provide feedback in a meaningful way.

o   Make sure expectations are realistic and attainable. Having ones that will stretch your team doesn't hurt, but achieving should be possible. Unrealistic expectations interfere with people's wellbeing.

o   Allow expectations to be flexible. If they're too rigid, it doesn't allow for unexpected change.

- What are some typical expectations teams have of their leaders?
    o   Clearly defined goals and objectives for success.
    o   Actions and words that are consistent.
    o   Growth and opportunities to challenge and inspire them in their careers.
    o   Their input and ideas are valued, so they feel they are contributing, involved, and respected.
    o   Be honest. No one likes being lied to; it's the quickest way to lose respect.
    o   Fight for your team and have their backs.
    o   Provide constructive feedback promptly.
    o   Encourage and praise them for their efforts.
- How are you going to determine achievable expectations for your team?
- How are you going to involve your team in setting these expectations?
- Your team has expectations of you as a leader.
    o   Do you know what they are?
    o   Engage with your team and have them tell you their expectations of you.

Reflection

- Sit down with your team and present your expectations of them and identify clear expectations they have of you as a leader.
- When presenting your expectations to the team, ask them if they require more information, if they make sense, are reasonable and achievable.

37 BE THE CALM IN THE STORM

Key Insights

- Being calm in the storm means not reacting to emotions and being committed to transparency. Be aware of how others are feeling, the environment, the situation, and our feelings so that we can respond versus react.
- You may fall apart and feel out of control, but your team needs to see you calm, focused, confident, and reasonable.
- Your leadership in a storm will define your team and their ability to trust you going forward. Whom they can trust in a crisis is vital to the success and growth of a team.
- A leader who can't be trusted when all is calm will not have the following and trust of the team during a crisis. It will become inherently impossible to overcome the situation.
- You don't need to fix everything and have all the answers! Allow your team to come up with solutions that can resolve the situation.
- Ensure the information you receive or provide is not inaccurate or misleading, as you want to combat misinformation and loss of trust.

Guidance

- How can a leader be intentional in being the calm in the storm?
    - o   Take a breath. Consciously be aware that you need to breathe.
    - o   Do not react; instead, take the approach of responding.
    - o   Become present to the reality and be slow to respond. Get out of your own head. Be slow to anger and quick to accept

the situation. Anger impairs a leader's judgement and can be all consuming.

o   Seek to understand the situation and ask questions to get the complete picture to ensure assumptions are not being made. This will set you up to be objective and make better decisions.

o   Be completely transparent and open with your team so they can rally around and provide real solutions to tackle the situation.

o   Provide accurate and unbiased information to fight the spread of misinformation.

o   It's okay to admit that you haven't been in this territory before. You will be more respected for it.

o   Seek advice/counsel to get outside input and insight.

o   Try to be proactive versus reactive despite already being in the storm.

•   How will staying calm impact the team?

o   A leader's behaviour and level-headedness trickles down to the team, and they will mimic the leader.

o   It increases performance, loyalty, and trust, as the team will know the leader stands behind them.

o   It allows the leader to think clearly and choose how they will respond appropriately. Despite things suddenly being out of control, they will regain some control.

o   It will strengthen and bond the team as everyone works together to tackle the situation.

o   It creates room for ingenuity and creativity from the team.

•   What analysis can a leader do to be better prepared for the next storm?

o   Evaluate the capabilities and skills required from the team to anticipate future storms and build their team accordingly. Future storms include changes in organization structure, market demands, and unknown surprises or changes.

o   Have a "lessons learned" discussion with the team to determine what worked, what did not work, and where there is opportunity to try something different.

o   Take time to reflect on their own responses as a leader, how the team reacted, and what can be done differently or what they can keep doing in the future.

Reflection

- Describe how your team responded when you reacted versus when you were the calm in the storm.
   o   What can you learn from the two different reactions?
- What can you work on doing now, when there is no storm, to build the trust of your team?
- What steps can you take to ensure you will respond appropriately during a crisis?

38   LEAD BY EXAMPLE

Key Insights

- How you lead will determine the effectiveness of you and your team.
- Leading by example demonstrates the excellence you want from your team, pushing them to be the best they can be.
- Your actions match your words, which inspires greatness.
- You will be viewed as respected and credible and not as a dictator or one who is shirking their responsibilities.
- Learn to delegate and not micro-manage.
- Authentic and ethical leaders will have strong teams.
- Employees/team members will be more forgiving and have grace for you when you fail.
- If you are inconsistent and hypocritical, people quickly notice and distrust what you have to offer.

Guidance

- What does it mean to lead by example?
  - o It means to lead individuals and influence their behaviours and attitudes by one's own behaviours instead of words. A leader will guide and inspire others to mirror their behaviours.
  - o It means showing the type of values and beliefs you stand by and are committed to, revealing your authentic self!
  - o Being the type of leader you would want to follow.
  - o A poor leader will be surrounded by conflict, as everyone wants to do their own thing and go their own way. Their actions will not match their words.
- What are the benefits of leading by example?

o Demonstrates and inspires individuals to create what is possible and to follow suit.

o It pushes you to learn and grow as you make mistakes, and how you handle them will be exhibited to the team.

o Sets clear expectations for the team and builds camaraderie.

o Provides opportunities to coach and mentor your team.

o Builds trust, respect, and credibility with the team.

o Encourages teamwork and the willingness to support each other, improving morale and creating a more cohesive team and organization.

- What are some ways to lead by example?

  o Admit when you don't know something and listen and learn from the team, as they may have the expertise to advise and resolve the issue. It also shows that you value your team.

  o Apologize when you've done something wrong, as it acknowledges that you're willing to learn from your mistakes and take ownership of them.

  o Ensure your words and your actions match. Deliver what you promise and involve your team in supporting you in achieving that promise.

  o Deal with conflict and roadblocks promptly to ensure progress continues to happen.

  o Be willing to roll up your sleeves and help with anything to support the team. This will help you understand what your team members do, increase morale, and make you more approachable.

  o Macro-managing will allow your team to be creative and think outside the box to get the job done, as you have provided a vision through your actions.

Reflection

- Assess areas and situations you can improve on to demonstrate leading by example to your team.
- Evaluate how your team has mirrored your behaviour, good or bad, and what needs to be done to continue or change that behaviour.

39   BE A FOLLOWER

Key Insights

- Being a leader-follower means finding value in your team, getting inspired by your team, and encouraging your team to communicate, brainstorm and be open.

"I must follow the people. Am I not their leader?"[1]
—Benjamin Disraeli, Former Prime Minister of the United Kingdom

- If you're a leader without following, you're a dictator.
- Provide awareness of other people's needs and potential.
- A team will follow someone whom they trust, who inspires hope and provides a stable environment.

"He who cannot be a good follower cannot be a good leader."[2] —Aristotle, Greek Philosopher

Guidance

- Why do leaders need to be followers at times?
  - o For leaders to be great, they must also be great followers.
  - o As leaders grow in their careers, they must focus on the bigger picture and trust their team with the day-to-day tasks.
  - o They view the team and organization differently as they interact with them.
  - o The focus is less on themselves and more on empowering people.

- o In a crisis, they take the time to empathize and actively listen to their employees and are better suited to support the team.
- What do leaders need to do to be a follower on their teams?
  - o Be humble, remove the ego, and know you are not the smartest person in the room. If you think you are, then you're in the wrong room.
  - o Put your team first!
  - o Empower your team to make decisions and support them through various situations.
  - o Be honest, brave, and respectful.
  - o Adjust communication style according to each team member's needs. This helps to inspire your team. It will also help you to share your thoughts and opinions effectively.
  - o Trust your people and follow their lead when they suggest or ask for help!
  - o This allows you to view the business differently and engage with your people.
- As leaders, there's a need to understand the different types of followers, the type you are and those on your team. Once you have identified the types of followers on the team, you can provide development and guidance to become effective team members. Ideally, you want people to become proactive, independent, and critical types.
  - o What are some types of followers?
    - Passive and Yes types—dependent on the leader, doing as they are told, not critical thinkers, and don't provide opposing opinions. They don't challenge their leader or provide alternative solutions, as they fear conflict.
    - Safety-First type—follow the path of least resistance and stay under the radar. They flip-flop with their opinions and thoughts.
    - Passive Independent Critical Thinkers type— disengaged, resist providing solutions or using their skills in supporting the team, negative and toxic.

- Proactive Independent Critical Thinkers type—tend to respect their leaders and challenge opposing views. They become trusted advisors, as they are engaged, consistent, produce quality, and are open-minded.
  o What type of follower are you?
  o What type of followers do you have on your team?

Reflection

- What areas can you work on to become a follower as a leader?
- Put this into practice. What was your team's reaction and response, verbally and nonverbally?

40 ADAPTABILITY

Key Insights

- It's imperative to be quick and nimble as a leader; change is inevitable.
- Change is not necessary—it is essential!
- How you respond and adapt to situations will determine how the team will function.
- Things don't always go as planned, and coming back from failure by learning from the mistakes will set you apart.
- Leaders unwilling to adapt will be seen as too rigid, costing the company's bottom line, as they will fall behind the curve.

Guidance

- Why is adaptability critical in leadership?
  - o Proactively finds solutions and learns from challenges.
  - o Can be innovative and adjust plans as changes come.
  - o Understands the different leadership styles and when to apply them to various situations.
  - o Increases the strength and success of the team.
- What are some skill sets of those who are adaptable and flexible?
  - o Self-management—the ability to control emotions, feelings, and activities.
  - o Decision making—some are easy decisions while others take time and analytical skills.
  - o Being calm in the face of difficulties.
  - o Optimistic—try to find the bright side of the situation, and it might open possible solutions that hadn't been considered.

o   Open to new ideas and changes. When you're positive, it opens the door to new ideas and changes that could take effect.

- What are some types of adaptive leadership styles?
    o   Strategic—a visionary who coordinates long-term growth, keeping the big picture in mind and developing strategies and goals to achieve it.
    o   Tactical—will make quick decisions and act with the current facts available.
    o   Change Management—is focused on the individuals and teams and creating change when required.
    o   Organizational—focuses on the organization and how the change will impact the environment while acting on potential issues.
- Describe a situation in which you had to adjust to changes you had no control over. How did you handle it?
- When did you have to adjust to a colleague's working style to complete a project or achieve your objectives?
- What has been the most stressful situation you have ever found yourself in at work? How did you handle it?
- Have you ever become frustrated or irritated because something kept changing? How did you handle it?

Reflection

- What areas can you improve on over the next week, month, and year around adaptability?

41 DECISION-MAKING/ DECISIVENESS

Key Insights

- Types of Decision Making
  - o Command—This is authoritative, the final decision made by the leader, and everyone is expected to accept and follow it.
  - o Consultation—You consult with your team and stakeholders and rationally decide what's in the best interest of the team/organization.
  - o Consensus—You take what most of the group wants to do. It may not be the most effective, as this is when groupthink happens and may not be in the best interest of the team/organization.
  - o Indecision—Not an option and does not gain respect or trust from your team, as it's paralysis by analysis.
- A leader who makes decisions shows they value and will have the team's back. They will garner respect and loyalty by being decisive. It will also increase productivity, improve morale, and save time.
- Decisiveness reduces conflict and confusion, as the team understands where you stand and your expectations.
- Indecisiveness, or taking too long to make decisions, can hinder one's career, as it becomes your reputation, and teams become frustrated and demotivated. You must evaluate if you should be in leadership.
- Timely decision-making sets you apart from your colleagues. It can mean the difference between being successful and being mediocre.

- For a leader to lead their team, they must make decisions. You must be brave; sometimes you will put your neck on the line.

Guidance

- What are some skills in making decisions?
  - o Logical Reasoning—evaluating the pros and cons of the potential solution.
  - o Creative Thinking—creating innovative solutions outside the standard tried and true practices.
  - o Critical Thinking—being well informed and gathering detailed information to see the big picture and the details and know the potential risks. It also involves healthy and productive conflict to improve the quality of your decision.
  - o Self-Awareness/Emotional Intelligence—understanding your emotions and expressing them measuredly, knowing the environment and what you have control over.
  - o Time Management—the timing of the decision allows for a thoughtful and coordinated approach. It's better to make a wrong decision than a good one too late. You still have time to fix it if it's a wrong decision.
- What are some critical steps for making a difficult decision?
  - o Discuss with the individuals the decision will affect and get potential solutions.
  - o Investigate the solutions in detail.
  - o Determine the potential alternatives.
  - o Identify and assess the risks.
  - o Select the best solution.
  - o Evaluate your plan.
  - o Communicate the decision and move forward.
- What happens when a leader has delayed or procrastinated in making a decision?
  - o Procrastination/avoidance can lead to increased stress and anxiety, frustration within the team, and demotivation.
  - o Procrastination is a coping mechanism to deal with stress. If you know the triggers, you can deal with them and bypass the procrastination.

- Can you make tough decisions? If not, should you be a leader?

Reflection

- Commit to "no decision-making avoidance" from this point forward.
- Document your answers and identify steps to change the following:
  - o Why did you delay or procrastinate a decision?
    - ▪ What were the triggers that caused the delay or procrastination?
    - ▪ What was the outcome?
  - o What is your typical approach to making decisions?
  - o How effective are you at making decisions?
  - o How do you respond to making immediate decisions?
  - o Have you been brave in making leadership decisions? If not, start now.

42 DELEGATING

Key Insights

- Be willing to delegate, as your presence will expand through your team.
- Be smart about delegating and assessing employee strengths and weaknesses.
- Know when to say "Yes," "No," or "Yes, if."
- Provide the whole picture and be transparent for your team to be successful.
- Allow your team to fail, and support them in figuring out how to be successful.

Guidance

- Why is delegating so crucial for teams?
  - o Empowerment of teams allows individuals to showcase their skill sets and value. They will be more invested and loyal as they are given the chance to take on new challenges.
  - o Expanding skills and building new skill sets challenge you and the team. It's not just the task individuals may be learning but how to communicate and work with others.
  - o Prioritization of tasks will help you as a leader determine what is important, critical, or nice to have and who has the skills on your team.
  - o A gift of freed-up time, as you can focus on areas and tasks only you can do.
- If you took time off, would your priorities progress?
  - o If you answered no, you are guilty of being too involved and holding on. As a leader, you need to expand your presence through your team.

- What can you do to improve how you delegate work?
    - o Check the person's skill set and expertise. Get feedback from others who have worked with them.
    - o Provide support and direction. Outline what needs to be done and why. Check on the team member regularly to assist with any questions and to remove roadblocks.
    - o Provide the whole picture as you know it, and don't hide anything; transparency and communication are key.
    - o Truly hand over the entire task. If the individual drops the ball somehow, don't take it back; help them pick it up and run with it again.
    - o Believe that the individual is capable and will get the job done.
    - o The job doesn't have to be completed the way you would do it as long it's done in the time required.
    - o Be discerning about what you take on, and match up demands with the skill set of your team members. Know when to say "Yes," "No," or "Yes, if."
        - ▪ "Yes," if your team has the skill set.
        - ▪ "No," if no one on your team has the skills or if there will be a more significant impact elsewhere.
        - ▪ "Yes, if," when skill sets are required that other teams or business units' skill sets are more suited to. Delegate to them. You don't need to do all the work but can support and encourage others.

Reflection

- Assess if you're willing and effective at delegating.
    - o If not, what is stopping you?
    - o What can you do to improve and put into practice delegation within your team?

43 DEFINING YOUR SUCCESS

Key Insights

- We can be the biggest roadblock to our success.
- Leaders are constantly being observed by their team and others. This requires them to be aware and carefully think through their behaviours and actions and lead by example.
- They must constantly learn, as success won't happen every time. When mistakes and failures happen, we truly learn and grow and appreciate when we are successful.
- There will always be bumps and curves in the road. How we handle and adapt will determine our success.

Guidance

- What does success look like for you and your team?
- What must you do differently to ensure you and your team are successful?
- What is your roadblock to being successful?
- What types of things can a leader do to achieve success?
  - o Get the right people on the team.
  - o Lead with confidence and never stop learning.
  - o Provide clear direction and be decisive.
  - o Inspire and guide others on your team to achieve their goals. Do not pigeonhole good resources, as this will create frustration and even cause them to leave the team/ organization.
  - o Be humble and remove pride and ego. You don't need to be the most intelligent person in the room or act like you are.
  - o Use open and transparent communication, and don't be afraid to say no.

o   Address issues/conflicts; do not avoid them.

o   Lead with your strengths and improve on those.

o   Know your weaknesses and surround yourself with people who are strong in these areas.

o   Be accessible and available to the team.

- What's the best way to learn and grow from the mistakes made on the journey to success?

    o   Acknowledge, accept it, and move forward. The first instinct is to deny it. Do not do that.

    o   Learn to forgive ourselves for the mistakes we made. We tend to berate and beat ourselves up. We need to learn to have grace for ourselves.

    o   When we fail on the outside, it helps us to succeed internally. It brings us to our knees and forces us to learn from that mistake to grow as an individual.

    o   Facing the result of mistakes, we don't give up but get up and move forward. It's the reversal of how we look at life from an internal rather than an external perspective.

- What are the benefits of not always being successful?

    o   Teaches humility, compassion, and empathy. It humanizes you as a leader, and there is no room for egos.

    o   It helps to teach us to manage expectations and know that everything is temporary.

    o   You can learn from mistakes. Don't let it stop you from trying again; you now have a framework of what worked and what didn't and can adjust accordingly.

    o   It will make you a better leader, as you must take the focus off yourself.

    o   It also creates an environment in which the teams see that they can make mistakes and that staying open to feedback is essential.

    o   It teaches us to survive failure and to persevere.

    o   Mistakes make us stronger and wiser if we allow them to.

- How does a leader determine if they are successful as a leader?

    o   Ask the team and yourself these questions:

        ▪   Does everyone know clearly what is expected of them?

- Has reinforcement of good work happened in the last week?
- Has everyone had the opportunity to do their best every day?
- Does everyone have what they need to do the job right (i.e., knowledge, software, and equipment)?
- Is development encouraged and recognized?

Reflection

- Analyze the following:
  o What can you do to encourage success on your team?
  o What areas of improvement or changes need to be made for you to be successful? How are you going to achieve these improvements?
  o What mistakes are you making as a leader, and how can you improve?

44 OWNERSHIP AND RESPONSIBILITY

Key Insights

- Acknowledge mistakes. We need to admit our mistakes and be okay with not being perfect. This shows humility, which will be respected more than denying them.
- People want to work for leaders who create a safe environment in which to make mistakes. We're all human.
- Bad leaders play the blame game instead of owning it.
- Ownership doesn't mean perfection. Being accountable means assuming responsibility for yourself, your work, and as a leader; you are accountable for your team's performance.
- Accountability moves ownership and responsibility from me to us and from the individual to the team. It will naturally happen from our colleagues around us.
- Trust in teams is built with accountability by their leader. If a leader takes responsibility for their work and actions, it creates greater confidence within the group that their leader will support them.
- Your team will take pride in their work if there is accountability and ownership. The quality and success of their work will show this.

Guidance

- How does a leader create an environment of ownership?
  o Empower the team to self-govern to focus on results.
  o Be transparent, especially on the desired outcome, and allow your team to do what they need to do to get there.

It may differ from how you would do it, but this allows for improvements and creativity.

o Encourage customer empathy.

■ Active listening to understand the desired outcome and priorities.

■ Be respectful.

■ Try and see it through the customer's eyes.

■ Make it your problem as well.

• How does a leader demonstrate that they are accountable?

o Defines expectations and outcomes without defining how it needs to be done. Allow the team to get from point A to point B without dictating how they do it.

o Does not micromanage.

o Sets the team up for success, removes roadblocks as required, and is willing to coach and encourage collaboration. No one wants to disappoint someone they report to or be the weakest link on the team.

o Acknowledges their mistakes and doesn't play the blame game.

o Demonstrates the behaviours the team should mirror.

Reflection

• What steps/actions must you take to show your team you are accountable and supportive of them?

• Identify and list the behaviours you need to change. Evaluate how your change in behaviour impacts your team over the next week and month.

45 DEALING WITH CHANGE

Key Insights

- People believe they will lose something of value or fear they will fail with the change. Provide them with a powerful reason/purpose for the change to create the energy and desire for the difference.
- Team engagement and support is a must when it comes to change, as there will be less resistance than to an imposed change.
- We can't own or control people or their responses. We can only own and control our response.

"You cannot shake hands with a clenched fist."[1]
—*Indira Gandhi, first female Prime Minister of India*

Guidance

- Why are people resistant to change?
  - o Lack of willingness to change.
  - o Scared of job loss.
  - o Viewed as a threat.
  - o Do not like change.
- What can a leader and team do to help people deal with the change that is coming?
  - o Address people's concerns and anxieties.
  - o Listen to what people fear and dig deeper.
  - o Careful planning and why. Communicate effectively with the various groups.

- o   Be adaptable and change direction if required to reach the end goal.
- How can a leader effectively bring change into the organization with their team?
  - o   Involve vital individuals from various business areas as Subject Matter Experts (SME) in determining the business requirements, success criteria, and benefits.
  - o   Get key individuals to highlight the resistors and identify the various stages of concern and how to respond with the correct information at the right time.
  - o   Get business units to be part of testing the product and being champions for their areas, especially those identified as resistant.
  - o   Training SMEs to be superusers to help train other individuals within their teams.
  - o   Train the resisters to be superusers. The more comfortable they are with the change, the more likely they'll be your biggest champions.
  - o   Train all the groups that will be affected by the change.
- What things does a leader need to know within the organization regarding change?
  - o   What is the current climate of the organization? How much change has the organization already experienced? There can be change fatigue when too many projects are going on in a short period of time.
  - o   How have past changes been made, and were they effective? What lessons can be learned from it?
  - o   Does this change align with the organization's business objectives? Why are they making this change? Are people onboard and in agreement with this change?
- How can a leader adjust their behaviour to deal with change?
  - o   Understand and know their vision.
  - o   Recognize the current reality within the organization, as this impacts the work and what will be accomplished.
  - o   Have a leadership advisor or accountability partner to support and encourage the change(s). They can also

highlight the roadblocks that others or you may be putting up to hinder your success. We can be our worst critics and biggest hindrances.

o   Move forward with experimenting and testing the change.

o   Take the time to evaluate and change course, remembering to celebrate success.

Reflection

•   What is a change that your team and specific individuals are struggling to accept? Document it and analyze:

o   What do you believe their issues are behind resisting the change?

o   How can you help them accept and move forward with the change?

o   Evaluate their progress over the next weeks and months.

INSIGHTS THAT CAN MAKE OR BREAK LEADERS

As leaders, we can create a team that functions exceptionally well; ultimately, how the team functions and the success/failure reflect on us as leaders, whether we like it or not. We must set the stage with a solid foundation, clear goals, and direction. This way, everyone knows where they're going and how to get there and will naturally come together based on the talents and abilities of the team.

"No man will make a great leader who wants to do it all himself or to get all the credit for doing it."[1] —Andrew Carnegie, Industrialist

46   BEING STRATEGIC

Key Insights

- Being strategic means having a common sense/logical approach to resolving any situation, no matter how complex and ambiguous.
- Be meaningful and purposeful in decision-making.
- Set a few limited goals, only one to three, as that is typically what people can handle.

> *"Leaders who know the few goals they want to pursue are better prepared to manage tough trade-offs, for example between: Short-term vs. long-term, Urgent vs. important, easy vs. difficult, comfortable vs. unpleasant."*[1]
> —*Marilyn Paul, Ph.D & David Peter Stroh*

Guidance

- What does it mean to be strategic?
  - o Create and clearly define the vision and goals that can be adapted to remain competitive. This involves long-term and short-term goals.
  - o Have a view of the future, not just the present. This will create excitement and inspire the team.
  - o Be transparent and consistent in communicating the organization's and team's vision and strategy. This may seem repetitive and boring, but people must hear it three times for something to sink in.
  - o Ensure accountability for yourself and your team to eliminate busy work. This enables clear roles and responsibilities for

the team members. It creates a sense of value, and people are willing to put more effort into what they feel is theirs to own.

o   Be willing to take calculated risks while minimizing risks and taking unnecessary gambles.

o   Focus on the bigger picture and get out of the weeds. Allow and trust your team be in the details.

- Why is Strategic Leadership important?

o   It ensures the organization/team has a clearly defined roadmap based on the vision and goals.

o   It promotes the continual growth of the organization/team.

o   Employees understand what they are working toward and where the company is heading.

- What are some types of strategic leadership?

o   Collaborative—There is an increase in innovation and creativity, as everyone has a chance to contribute. They can quickly build trust and respect from the team, improving solution options. Decision-making is slowed due to trying to involve everyone's opinions. This will also create more conflict and tension in the team. There also tends to be less structure and follow-through.

o   Directive—This is conventional leadership and can be military-like. They can produce the results as quickly as possible. They are clear in their communication, use a straightforward approach, and will use their authority in a crisis to make decisions. Their teams know the direction and are not left with ambiguity. The Business Units may not feel like their ideas and solutions are valued, which can be demotivating.

o   Visionary—Will motivate and inspire the team so they can dream big. They aren't afraid to fail, will learn from their mistakes, and are ambitious. They can be narrow-minded depending on their beliefs and priorities. They will discard the conventional and will settle for nothing but the best.

o   These leadership types can blend, but typically one is more dominant than the others.

- How does a leader develop a strategic mindset?
    - o Question the status quo. Evaluate the past and present, successes and failures, and apply those learnings to now and in the future.
    - o Take risks and do not follow the norm. There are always innovations, technology, and ideas, so be open to the possibilities and potential failures and learn from them.
    - o Be open to and understand opposing arguments and ideas, as it will give you a better insight into the big picture.
    - o Once the big picture has been developed, it doesn't mean it's one and done. You need to go back and each week be purposeful in reflecting and reviewing it. This is a time to evaluate new information and trends, adjusting accordingly.

Reflection

- Identify your strategic leadership type, What can you do to balance the other two types to balance out your dominant type?

47 CRITICAL THINKING

Key Insights

- Critical thinkers are individuals who have foresight and practical problem-solving skills. This ability is necessary for good decisions to be made. They are critical, creative, and collaborative in their thinking.
- Critical thinkers are sought after, as they provide thoughtful and insightful questions and solutions.
- Curiosity does not kill the cat! Asking questions and removing biases will set you up for increased confidence and success.
- There's a need to see the logical relationship between thoughts and ideas and recognize mistakes in reasoning.
- This discipline can be developed, and your team will follow as they learn from you as the leader.

Guidance

- What qualities/skills are required to be a critical thinker?
  - Ask important questions, raise issues, and provide potential solutions.
  - Be observant and mindful of their surroundings and people to foresee potential issues or problems before they happen.
  - Be able to gather and interpret relevant and essential information and data to solve problems and creatively develop potential solutions.
  - Effectively explain and discuss various topics and actively listen.
  - Come to logical and rational decisions.
- How can one develop critical thinking skills?

o Self-Awareness—understand who you are in your values, morals, beliefs, thought processes, strengths, weaknesses, and perspectives.

o Observation/Foresight—analyze your decision by looking at the pros and cons, how it will impact others, and how others will potentially respond.

o Research/gather and evaluate new and current information, ensuring it is from credible sources. New information needs to be vetted and assessed to understand its motivation.

o Decisiveness—develop your opinion with confidence in the outcome.

o Put yourself in situations that allow you to develop and practise these skills, such as group collaborations, new experiences, journaling, and solving familiar issues.

o What are some question types in critical thinking?

o Open-ended—facilitate discussions and more thought-provoking answers.

o Closed-ended—there are only two possible answers.

o Recall and process questions—a look back on previous experiences and outcomes.

o Factual—answers are based on facts or awareness.

o Evaluation—analysis is done from various perspectives before answering.

• What are some examples of questions to get the information needed?

o What is the issue exactly?

o How is this issue like other issues? How is it NOT like other issues?

o Are we taking a simplistic approach to a complex problem?

o Are we making this solution more complex than it should be?

o Are the standard approaches failing? If so, what needs to be changed to be successful?

o Am I missing something that others are seeing?

o What happens if we take a portion out of the situation?

o What happens if we add a factor to the situation?

Reflection

- What areas of your critical thinking skills do you need to improve upon?
- What tangible steps are you going to take to improve?
- Consider asking your leadership advisor/accountability partner to support and guide you to improve your critical thinking, or find someone solid in their critical thinking skills to observe and provide you with their insights.

48 CREATIVE THINKING

Key Insights

- Creativity helps us navigate change, especially in a world of constant change.
- In large corporations, leaders are taught to think linearly, unlike start-up company leaders, who must think innovatively.
- The world is changing rapidly and so must corporations' and leaders' responses.
- Break the routine of redundancy and be aware that success can create repetitiousness. Success becomes the comfort zone, as it's believed that it worked once, so it will work again, which is not always true. Instead, there's a need to continue pushing the limits and trying creative and new ways.

Guidance

- What is creative thinking?
  - o Creating and recognizing innovative solutions to complex or changing situations/problems, pushing the limits.
- What are some qualities of a creative thinker?
  - o Has the courage to make tough decisions and admit when wrong.
  - o Strength and bravery under pressure and determination in defeat.
  - o Drops the ego and pettiness; no need to be the most intelligent person in the room. Asks questions as well as gains insight and feedback from those around them.
  - o Open-mindedness for new ideas, as thinking outside the box inspires others.

- o Will often contradict themselves and others to question assumptions.
- o Gets out of their comfort zone and goes against expectations.
- o Has high standards and personal ethics and sticks to their convictions.
- What can a leader do to develop their creative thinking skills?
  - o Identify the problem and gather information/data on it.
  - o Brainstorm using mind maps to flush out the ideas and questions, which will drive out potential solutions. Push yourself outside of your comfort zone when coming up with solutions.
  - o Evaluate solutions and which ones make sense in resolving the situation.
  - o Implement the solution and adapt as you roll it out.
  - o Fight the fear of failure and overcome a negative attitude.
- What are some benefits of having creative thinking on teams?
  - o Teams are more collaborative, which involves speaking up and listening to each other.
  - o Attracts more diversity on the team, leading them to challenge and debate each other healthily.
  - o Creates a team that thrives and adapts quickly and confidently to change.
  - o Creative thinking on teams will challenge the norm of the organization, people, and services. This will increase productivity, attract the best people, and produce better products/services in an ever-changing environment.

Reflection

- Identify what you need to work on to improve your creative skills as a leader.
- Looking back at past situations, what could you have done differently to encourage creative thinking?

49 VISION, MISSION, AND VALUES

Key Insights

- Creates a solid foundation and supports your team with clear expectations and direction.
- No one enjoys ambiguity!
- Creates a purposeful direction for the organization/team and supports the strategy.
- Guides behaviours and decisions for a common goal.

Guidance

- What are the roles of vision, mission, and values?
  - o Vision supports the strategy of the organization/team. It describes the futuristic purpose of what the organization is to become.
  - o Mission helps prioritize the task and activities, which provides a framework for decision-making. It's the organization/team's reason/purpose for being.
  - o Values are what the organization/team creates; it is a code of ethics.
- How do vision and mission influence your leadership abilities?
  - o Provides a standard to monitor performance, progress, and success.
  - o Motivates your team, as they have clear direction and guidelines. Ambiguity is removed.
  - o Sets a solid and sound foundation from which your team can grow and succeed.
  - o Supports creativity, empowerment, and proactive action.
  - o Helps in attracting the right talent for your team.

- As a leader, do you have a vision, mission, and values for your team that match or support the corporate ones?
  - o Does your team know what they are?
  - o Do they need to be adjusted to better support the organization? If so, how and what needs to change?
  - o If you do not have these, why not?

Reflection

- Work with your team to build the vision, mission, and values if you have yet to do so. If you need to adjust the team's vision, mission, and values, do it as a team-building activity. This will create buy-in and build your team culture moving forward.

50 MEETINGS

Key Insights

- Know the purpose of the meeting and what outcomes you want to see from it.
- Have an agenda.
- Ensure you have the right people in the meeting to achieve the expected outcome.
- When decisions must be made, allow time for healthy debate/conflict. This helps to build a stronger team.
- Create a parking lot to manage off-topic items, but make sure you follow up on these items.
- Manage the clock so meetings end on time, and use everyone's time effectively.
- Make sure meetings aren't happening for the sake of happening. People's time is valuable and should be used effectively.
- Engage everyone who is attending the meeting. This can be done by asking attendees who have yet to comment on topics for their thoughts or opinions.
- Always bring your A-Game to every meeting—be present, focused, and prepared.
- Facilitating a meeting means guiding the conversation but allowing the participants to speak.
- Online meetings are more complex than in-person.

Guidance

- What can a leader do to facilitate a productive meeting?
  - o Define the purpose and agenda for the meeting, allowing the invitees to prepare.

- o Invite the right people to the meeting, especially when decisions must be made.
- o Allow time for discussion and initiate the conversation by asking questions.
- o Be present in the meeting; this may mean getting someone else to take notes, closing your laptop, and shutting off your phone.
- o Ensure you start and end on time.
- o Read the room and know your audience.
- o Keep the meeting moving and put ideas into a parking lot if they distract from the purpose of the meeting.
- What are some examples of meeting etiquette?
  - o Have a set of ground rules, such as being on time, use of laptops and cell phones, and interrupting while someone is speaking or waiting until the end.
  - o Virtual meetings—way easier to be distracted. There's a need to make a rule that people must have their cameras on, ask specific questions, and direct them at the individuals to ensure engagement.
- How can one engage each team member in the meetings?
  - o Go around the table and ask each person what they have completed, what they will be working on next, and if there are any wins, risks, issues, or concerns.
  - o Watch body language: it tells you so much.
  - o Make sure everyone participates and get them involved.
- How can a leader motivate the team in a long meeting (2+ hrs.)?
  - o Bring squish toys that they can pick up and play with. This allows the individual to step back and refocus. They will likely come back with some great ideas.
  - o Set the meeting title as a question to keep people engaged. Have an agenda. Don't make it easy for the individuals just to show up.
  - o Be on time for meetings and end on time. Respect everyone's schedule.
- How effective are your meetings?
- What can you do to improve your meetings?

Reflection

- Implement different techniques in running your meetings and watch how your team responds.
- Create and communicate the meeting etiquette that everyone agrees to with the team.

51 BE ORGANIZED/ TIME MANAGEMENT

Key Insights

- Respect other people's time by being purposeful and on time.
- Refrain from allowing emails, meetings, and other work to consume you and take away from supporting your team. Plan time for your team.
- Put your phone away and be present, especially in meetings and discussions.
- Time management and organization skills are disciplines. We need to be wise and make difficult decisions with our valuable time, recognizing that it doesn't mean doing more with less.
- Understand what you are wasting your time on and what changes need to be made to your organizational methods.

Guidance

- What are some of the biggest time wasters?
    - o Micro-managing, as you stop people from growing when you get involved where you shouldn't. Be a macro-manager instead.
    - o In crisis management, be proactive versus reactive. This doesn't mean that crises won't arise on occasion, but those should be few and far between, not daily or weekly.
    - o Failing to delegate; trust your team. If you can't trust your team, then you need to re-evaluate yourself as a leader and your team.

o Poor planning and focusing on unnecessary tasks or urgent items versus important tasks. Set aside specific times to work on essential tasks and stop doing busy work.

o Implementing versus doing analysis; creating inefficiencies. Be systematic in your approach.

o The lack of standards, policies, and procedures creates an environment of inconsistency, chaos, and instability. Be methodical, reasonable, and structured with room for out-of-the-box creativity.

o Procrastination can create unnecessary stress and ineffective work. Set realistic timelines for yourself to complete tasks.

• What are some tools to help a leader with time management and organization?

o To-do lists allow you to cross things off and see what you accomplish, focusing on one task at a time.

o Stop wasting other people's time and your own with unnecessary meetings and tasks.

o Set short-term and long-term priorities, ensuring there is room to add unexpected requests. Even prioritize your emails and ensure they are to the point and precise, reducing confusion and the need to have additional follow-up emails or meetings.

o Allow time to reflect on what needs to be done and what you have accomplished.

o Refrain from overcomplicating things. Keep it simple!

o Delegate and empower your team. Do not own everything; you are only one person. Don't try to be the hero; allow your team to be the heroes.

o Know when to stop with a task or a procedure. Use the Pareto Principle of 80 percent of results coming from just 20 percent of the effort, and don't try to achieve perfection; figure out when something is good enough.

o Prioritize your tasks and areas of focus each week and for each day.

o   Ensure your desk and emails are organized to access crucial information, especially in times of urgency, easily. This habit will save you loads of time in the future.

o   Get comfortable saying no. Take on a manageable amount, as you want to keep your commitments and produce quality. Take on enough that it will challenge you to grow.

- How can a leader qualify if a priority/task request is a "Yes" or a "No"?

o   Is this a SMART Request? Has the requester outlined precise details and standards and made the request achievable and realistic with clear, attainable dates?

o   Review with your resources if they have the time required to perform the task as requested.

o   If unable to achieve what is requested, negotiate with an alternative to meet their needs.

o   If there are trade-offs, clarify with the requester and work together to develop alternative solutions.

Reflection

- List the strategies or activities that you will do this week to improve your organization and time management. Evaluate at the end of the week and month any improvements.
- Identify what you need to change when it comes to saying no. Practise saying no over the next week and month.

52 NEGOTIATIONS

Key Insights

- In leadership, you will constantly be negotiating what is key and how effective you are at it.
- Negotiation is a skill that can be learned and practised. There is no science to it, but it will become an art.
- Negotiations are about understanding each side's desired outcome and moving toward a solution that benefits everyone. It's not a one-sided situation unless you make it so.
- Negotiations will fail, so stay calm and walk away gracefully to ensure you don't burn bridges.

Guidance

- What can leaders do to support the negotiation process?
  o Be prepared and anticipate potential roadblocks—research so that you can provide facts and avoid potential conflict.
  o Have realistic expectations by identifying what potentially would be your ideal, natural, and worse-case outcomes.
  o Lead the discussions so that you can drive the direction of the conversation and negotiations.
  o Actively listen to the other party to show you understand their points.
  o Ask open-ended questions, as those require explanations versus definitive answers.
  o Be comfortable in the silence and use it to reflect on how negotiations are going and get your emotions in check.
  o Do not act arrogant or aggressively; be respectful. Check your attitude and emotions! Be self-aware, as this will impact the negotiation process. Stay calm!

- o Seek advice and feedback to help negotiate perspectives, which can help build long-lasting business relationships.
- o Avoid conflict by adjusting your strategy and staying adaptable.
- o Know when to compromise and stop! It will increase respect and save time; you want to ensure you develop long-term relationships by not burning bridges. There comes a point where it's just nitpicking and becomes a time waster.
- When do negotiation skills come into play as a leader?
  - o Dealing with vendors, suppliers, and clients.
  - o Business units within the organization.
  - o Team members with their time, priorities, pay increases, etc.
  - o When dealing with conflict or complaints.
- What are negotiation styles?
  - o Competition—You are "in it to win it" at all costs and couldn't care less about the outcome for the other side.
  - o Collaboration—You want a win-win outcome and create creative and innovative solutions.
  - o Compromise—You want both parties to sacrifice, and needs are only partially met.
  - o Accommodation—You will lose, as you want to ensure the relationship with the other side and avoid conflict.
  - o Avoidance—You like to remain neutral and avoid any tension or conflict.
- Which style do you fall into?
- What are some required negotiation skills?
  - o Persuasion—the ability to influence people using facts and convincing arguments.
  - o Effective communication—the ability to use written, nonverbal, and clear verbal communication styles.
  - o Planning—the ability to process and identify goals, desired outcomes, and potential roadblocks.
  - o Flexibility—the ability to quickly change and adjust to develop a new strategy to ensure progress continues with the negotiations.

o   Problem-solving—the ability to determine why an issue has arisen and how to resolve it creatively.

Reflection

- Identify and list your strengths and weaknesses in negotiations. What changes are you going to make to improve your negotiation skills?

INFORMATION
TIDBITS

"Be careful who you let on your ship because some people will sink the whole ship just because they can't be the captain." —Unknown

TIDBITS

Business Storytelling

- People naturally gravitate to exciting and fun stories, as they are creatures of emotions and logic. Stories are easy to remember, impactful, and help build trust.
- Being able to tell a story with facts and figures will reach people, but only after they have heard a good story will they genuinely pay attention.
- When story telling, make sure the story is engaging (have a hook) and contains authentic narrative with a clear outcome/ message. Be consistent and make your audience part of the story.
- Don't make yourself the hero in the story but be genuine. Share stories that tell people more about who you are.

Micromanagement

- The constant and unnecessary control over the team and activities.
- You may be a micromanager if you (this is not an exhaustive list):
  o Constantly check on the team's activities.
  o Have to be part of every meeting with the team.
  o Require frequent status updates/reports.
  o Never see initiative or new ideas come from the team.
  o Never are satisfied with the work done.
  o Believe you know it all and know best.
  o Experience high turnover on your team, and all your best resources have left.

- o Refuse to allow the team to talk to anyone above your level without you.
- o Do not allow for potential changes in ways of doing things.
- o Estimate time tasks will take for your team.
- o Demand that everything requires your approval.
- o Want to do it all and don't want to delegate.
- o Never experience the team coming to you for guidance or with questions.
- o Focus on the details instead of the big picture.
- o Re-do tasks or take tasks away from the team.
- o Contact the team outside of office hours regularly.
- o Need to be copied on all emails.

Leading Hybrid Environments

- Leaders must recognize and accept that a hybrid workforce is the new reality and figure out how they are going to adapt to it.
- Hybrid environments require resilient leaders who are able to reflect and assess themselves, continually grow, adapt to change, and know how to build relationships.
- Leaders need to understand their weaknesses, as the hybrid model is going to highlight them.
- Leaders are having to adapt their leadership styles to accommodate the various personalities, work styles, and situations. They are also having to be flexible in changing processes and procedures that are not working in a hybrid environment.
- Communication must be done through several different channels to ensure the team is getting what they need, such as email, video conferencing, instant messaging, phone calls.
- There's a greater need for trust and accountability for leaders and team members. Team members must manage their own time and tasks with the flexibility to work the way that works best for them. Leaders must recognize results versus work hours. Leaders are having to hold them accountable by providing constructive feedback and guidance.
- Creativity in building a cohesive team is required for leaders, especially when the team is in different locations. Host virtual

team meetings and events, or have spontaneous, friendly conversations.

- Empowerment is key for leaders, as they must allow their teams to share in responsibility and decision making.
- Leaders must be careful not to favour those individuals on the team who show up to the office versus those working in other locations. It's easier to build relationships with those that are present, and a leader must be intentional in building relationships virtually and creating an inclusive environment. Leaders need to be cognizant and intentional about who they promote within the organization, as it is easier to promote who you have a relationship with versus those that are at a distance.
- Hybrid environments make it easier to access the leader and the team, as everyone is attached to their technology. There's a greater need to ensure wellbeing and balance.

Personality Types

The below are generalizations, and we can have some characteristics more than others.

- Introvert—gets their energy from spending time alone.
- Extrovert—gets their energy from being around people.
- Ambivert—is a balance of introvert and extrovert traits and personality.
- Omnivert—is the extreme of both introverts and extroverts and is unpredictable, as they will act differently depending on the situation.
- Amiable—gets along with everyone, patient, quiet, well-balanced, and witty but can avoid conflict and be stubborn and selfish.
- Analytical—serious, deep, thoughtful, organized, perfectionist, with a dry sense of humour but can come across as negative and critical.
- Driver—dynamic, active, sees the big picture, visionary, and decisive. Still, they are not detail oriented but struggle with admitting when they are wrong; they may not evaluate the

consequences of their decisions, they lack compassion, and can struggle with pride.

- Expressive—loves to have fun, generous, has a sense of humour, and wants to be involved in everything, but can be disorganized, loud, and extremely talkative.

Workplace Bullying

- Bullying isn't just happening to kids at school or on social media. It is common in the workplace.
- You might be considered a bully if you:
  o Yell, belittle, and/or give silent treatment—This is unacceptable behaviour. It creates fear and humiliates the team, especially when they've made a mistake or haven't met your expectations.
  o Super micromanage—You inform your team that they can't do their jobs. This will severely decrease morale and increase turnover.
  o Argue to win at the cost of everyone else.
  o Don't think about what you're saying to others and how it might impact their feelings.
  o Quick to anger if people don't get in line quickly or don't see your point of view.
  o Become indignant and shut down if you don't agree with or like what someone is saying, especially when you don't think their views matter.
  o Constantly put team members down instead of praising them to management. This says more about your lack of self-worth and inability to be a team player.
  o Alienate or isolate individuals and make them feel unwelcome. You need to evaluate why you're doing this and determine if it's due to your own insecurities.
  o Provide only negative performance reviews and no positive feedback.

Maturity and Growth as a Leader

Maturity and Growth Evaluation Checklist:
- Are you standing alone for what is right?
- Are you running away from the pressure?
- Are you fearful of intimidation and worry?
- Do you have friends who will stand by you through thick or thin?
- Are you caring for others?
- Are you humble in mind when you give and focus on others?
- Have you taken the chip off your shoulders?
- Can you take the brunt without retaliating, especially when there is injustice?
- Can you control your tongue?
- Do you refrain from gossiping, telling confidential information, and passing judgement without all the facts?
- Do a checkpoint at the end of a week, a month, and a year to see how you have changed.

Common Mistakes Leaders Make

- Believing that you must know it all and do it all. You don't need to know everything; that's what the team is for. This also helps to build the team when they're part of the discussions and decisions; otherwise, you're stuck with being part of every meeting and discussion. That's a complete waste of your time and creates frustration on the team.
- Managing tasks and events at the cost of leading people. Get out of the weeds. Look at the bigger picture. Stop micromanaging your team.
- Refraining from delegating and trusting your team to do what is required to excel.
- Inability to clearly define goals and expectations.
- Being reactive instead of proactive. Constantly putting out fires instead of stepping back and getting a high-level view and determining where the potential issues could be.

- Being too "hands-on" or "hands-off." Find the balance to empower your team and develop their skill sets to meet the expectations.
- Having no time for your team. Block time in your calendar for your team and have an open-door policy so they can come to you when they need support and guidance.
- Being too friendly. There needs to be a balance of being a friend and being a boss.
- Confusion about the motivations and needs of the team; it is not exclusively money.
- Actions and words do not match, creating an environment of mistrust and disrespect for you as a leader.
- Not recognizing that your responsibilities change as you grow in your leadership roles, and a new skill set might be required to perform that role.
- Key traits to combat the common mistakes:

  o Take responsibility and accountability for your mistakes.
  o Lose the ego, deliver as promised, and refrain from pushing your agenda.
  o Rely on and trust the team and their expertise and be an expert at being a leader. Wait to provide guidance.
  o Acknowledge your fear and vulnerability and boldly lead your team. They will follow and help identify and support the issues that arise. You will be greatly respected for being honest.
  o Involve the team in identifying the root cause and solutions to the roadblocks. This may mean thinking outside the box and being innovative in solutions. Do not give up, even if it seems impossible.
  o Remove the roadblocks/barriers to ensure that the team can focus on the tasks they need to complete and so that you can help deal with the issues they face.

Additional Reading Sources

- *Boundaries* by Dr. Henry Cloud and Dr. John Townsend
- *Crucial Conversations* by Kerry Patterson, Joseph Grenny, Ron McMillan, Al Switzler
- *The Definitive Book of Body Language* by Barbara Pease and Allan Pease
- *Emotional Intelligence* by Daniel Goleman
- *The Five Dysfunctions of a Team* by Patrick Lencioni
- *Life Is 10% What Happens to You and 90% How You React* by Charles R. Swindoll
- *Never Split the Difference* by Chris Voss
- *Snakes in Suits* by Paul Babiak, Ph.D., and Robert D. Hare, Ph.D.
- *True North: Emerging Leader Edition* by Bill George and Zach Clayton

ACKNOWLEDGEMENTS

Thank you to my parents, Gordon and Nettie, and sister, Kristy, for always encouraging me and asking how things are going. Thanks for believing in me when I didn't believe in myself. Thank you for being so proud!

To Darlene Starr, for holding me accountable weekly and pushing me out of my comfort zone to finish this project. I've loved all our amazing discussions. Your wisdom and insight have been invaluable. This book would not have gotten done without you!

To Barry Henderson for pushing me to write this book and being willing to review and edit it. You brought a different perspective and encouraged me out of my comfort zone.

Thank you to all my family and friends who encouraged and cheered me on in this journey. There are so many of you!

NOTES

Introduction

1. Kizer, Kristin. 2023. "36 Powerful Leadership Statistics [2021]: Things All Aspiring Leaders Should Know—Zippia." Zippia. February 9, 2023. https://www.zippia.com/advice/leadership-statistics/.
2. Folkman, Joseph. n.d. "The Shocking Statistics behind Uninspiring Leaders." Forbes. Accessed January 29, 2024. https://www.forbes.com/sites/joefolkman/2018/11/20/the-shocking-statistics-behind-uninspiring-leaders/?sh=49e409be2b65.
3. Kizer, Kristin. 2023. "36 Powerful Leadership Statistics [2021]: Things All Aspiring Leaders Should Know – Zippia." Zippia. February 9, 2023. https://www.zippia.com/advice/leadership-statistics/.
4. Ibid.
5. Hurley, Robert. 2014. "The Decision to Trust." Harvard Business Review. August 21, 2014. https://hbr.org/2006/09/the-decision-to-trust.
6. Wittenberg, Anka. 2015. "The Business Impact of Authentic Leadership." Entrepreneur. April 20, 2015. https://www.entrepreneur.com/leadership/the-business-impact-of-authentic-leadership/245111.
7. Bistrisky, Eileen. 2023 Email, October 5, 2023.

Characteristics of an Authentic Leader

1. George, Bill, and Zach Clayton. 2022. *True North, Emerging Leader Edition: Leading Authentically in Today's Workplace.* 3rd ed. Nashville, TN: John Wiley & Sons.

2 Authentic Self

1. Adams, John Quincy. n.d. "Inaugural Address." Ucsb.edu. Accessed May 23, 2024. https://www.presidency.ucsb.edu/documents/inaugural-address-25.

3 Playing to Your Strengths

1. James Freeman Clarke. 1874. *Common-Sense in Religion: A Series of Essays,* 339. James R. Osgood and Company.

7 Boundaries

1. Taken from *Boundaries.* 207-208. by Dr. Henry Cloud & Dr. John Townsend Copyright © 1992 by Dr. Henry Cloud & Dr. John Townsend. Used by permission of HarperCollins Christian Publishing.

9 Dealing with Hurt

1. Mulla, Zainab. 2014. "Indira Gandhi's 97th Birth Anniversary: Top 20 Quotes of India's Only Woman Prime Minister." November 19, 2014. https://www.india.com/viral/indira-gandhis-97th-birth-anniversary-top-20-quotes-of-indias-only-woman-prime-minister-197900/.

Leadership Traits to Be Authentic

1. Asl, Farshad. 2016. *The No Excuses Mindset: A Life of Purpose, Passion, and Clarity.* 106. Author Academy Elite.

13 Integrity

1. Words framed at the Connecticut Mark Twain Memorial Hartford. 1901, February 16, 1901.
2. Williams, P., & Denney, J. 2008. Chapter 3. *In Souls of Steel: How to Build Character in Ourselves and Our Kids*, 38. essay, FaithWords.

14 Vulnerability

1. "Vulnerability: Why It Is a Leadership Strength, Not a Weakness? - Excel." n.d. Www.excel-Communications.com. https://www.excel-communications.com/blog/vulnerability-why-it-is-a-leadership-strength-not-a-weakness.

15 Self-Discipline

1. Gourani, Soulaima. 2024. "Why Discipline Outshines Motivation for Effective Leadership." Forbes. January 1, 2024. https://www.forbes.com/sites/soulaimagourani/2024/01/01/why-discipline-outshines-motivation-for-effective-leadership/?sh=4fe94c6829bd.

22 Self-Awareness

1. Arruda, William. n.d. "Why Self Awareness Is the Most Important Skill for Hybrid Leadership." *Forbes*. https://www.forbes.com/sites/williamarruda/2023/01/10/why-self-awareness-is-the-most-important-skill-for-hybrid-leadership/?sh=12d16d75654f.
2. A Better Return on Self-Awareness." 2021. Kornferry.com. Korn Ferry. April 15, 2021. https://www.kornferry.com/insights/briefings-magazine/issue-17/better-return-self-awareness.

3. "Women Poised to Effectively Lead in Matrix Work Environments, Hay Group Research Finds." 2012. Www.businesswire.com. March 27, 2012. https://www.businesswire.com/news/home/20120327005180/en/Women-Poised-to-Effectively-Lead-in-Matrix-Work-Environments-Hay-Group-Research-Finds.

24 Creating a Positive Environment

1. Swindoll, Charles R. 2023. Life Is 10% What Happens to You and 90% How You React. Nashville, TN: Thomas Nelson.

26 Motivating People and Team Building

1. Bersin, Josh. 2013. "Employee Retention Now a Big Issue: Why the Tide Has Turned." Linkedin.com. 2013. https://www.linkedin.com/pulse/20130816200159-131079-employee-retention-now-a-big-issue-why-the-tide-has-turned/.

29 The Reality of Office Politics

1. Dictionary, Merriam Webster's Collegiate. 2014. *Office Politics*. Springfield, MA: Merriam-Webster.

Communication

1. Gallo, Carmine. 2022. "How Great Leaders Communicate." *Harvard Business Review*, November 23, 2022. https://hbr.org/2022/11/how-great-leaders-communicate.

32 Reading Body Language

1. Mehrabian, Albert, and Morton Wiener. 1967. "Decoding of Inconsistent Communications." *Journal of Personality and Social Psychology* 6 (1): 109–14. https://doi.org/10.1037/h0024532.
2. Mehrabian, Albert, and Susan R. Ferris. 1967. "Inference of Attitudes from Nonverbal Communication in Two

Channels." *Journal of Consulting Psychology* 31 (3): 248–52. https://doi.org/10.1037/h0024648.

3. Pease, Allan, and Barbara Pease. 2011. *The Definitive Book of Body Language: The Hidden Meaning behind People's Gestures and Expressions.* New York: Bantam Dell.

Influencing the Direction of the Team

1. Simic, Zora. 2021. "How Eleanor Roosevelt Reshaped the Role of First Lady and Became a Feminist Icon." The Conversation. June 25, 2021. https://theconversation.com/how-eleanor-roosevelt-reshaped-the-role-of-first-lady-and-became-a-feminist-icon-156295.

39 Be a Follower

1. "The Work of Leadership." 2016. Icma.org. December 12, 2016. https://icma.org/articles/pm-magazine/work-leadership#:~:text=Interestingly%2C%20versions%20of%20this%20quote.

2. Schroeder, Bernhard. 2019. "To Be A Great Leader, Learn How to Be A Great Follower: The Four Rules of Following." Forbes. December 5, 2019. https://www.forbes.com/sites/bernhardschroeder/2019/12/05/to-be-a-great-leader-learn-how-to-be-a-great-follower-the-four-rules-of-following/?sh=218974ee7325.

45 Dealing with Change

1. Mulla, Zainab. 2014. "Indira Gandhi's 97th Birth Anniversary: Top 20 Quotes of India's Only Woman Prime Minister." November 19, 2014. https://www.india.com/viral/indira-gandhis-97th-birth-anniversary-top-20-quotes-of-indias-only-woman-prime-minister-197900/.

Insights That Can Make or Break Leaders

1. November 15, 1975. Section: Weekend, Helping hand, Quote Deseret News (Salt Lake City, Utah: 1975), W3.

46 Being Strategic

1. Paul, Marilyn, and David Peter Stroh. 2015. "Managing Your Time as a Leader—the Systems Thinker." The Systems Thinker. November 8, 2015. https://thesystemsthinker.com/ managing-your-time-as-a-leader/.

Manufactured by Amazon.ca
Acheson, AB

14286369R00096